THE GOLD GUIDES

Giuliano Valdes

PRAGUE

A COMPLETE GUIDE
TO THE CITY

Photography by Andrea Pistolesi

BONECHI

HOW TO USE THIS GUIDE

This guide is based on an innovative concept. Wherever the visitor begins his tour of the city, he can choose the places he wishes to visit without having to follow a set itinerary.

With this aim, the city has been divided into 12 areas, each of which contains one of the important sights which make up the obligatory stops for anyone visiting Prague. Other sights in the immediate vicinity, included in the area, can be visited according to time available and personal interest.

The areas have been arranged in the guide in such a way as to follow on geographically, so that those who wish to can use them to devise an itinerary through the city. However, in whatever order the visitor decides to see the city, this guide is easy to consult precisely because its main feature is to grant the visitor freedom of choice and movement, thanks also to the general map included with the guide, and to the specific area plans.

In the area plans, the symbol ▸ next to a caption means that this monument or place is described or mentioned in the guide. The symbol ▸▸ means that there is also a photograph of that particular sight.

Printed in Italy by Centro Stampa Editoriale Bonechi

Text: *Giuliano Valdes*
Editing: *Editing Studio, Pisa*
Translation: *Sarah Thompson*
Art Work: *Franco Filiberto*
Paging: *Studio Graffiti, Pisa*
Cartography: *Bernardo Mannucci*

Photographic References: photographs are the property of the
Casa Editrice Bonechi archives and were taken by Andrea Pistolesi.

Giuliano Valdes - Editing Studio, Pisa - photos pp. 26, 44 (lower part),
47 (lower part), 50 (upper part), 53, 56, 57 (upper part), 60, 67, 68, 70 (upper part),
72, 78, 86 (lower part), 89.

• • •
ISBN 88 - 8029 - 621 - 3

INTRODUCTION AND HISTORICAL BACKGROUND

T he Magical City", "The Golden City", "The City of a Hundred Towers", the "Paris of the East"; these are just some of the most common definitions adopted by popular tourist publications when talking about Prague, a city of around 1,200,000 inhabitants and, since 1st January 1993, capital of the Czech Republic, as well as capital of central Bohemia. The city offers a wealth of architectural, artistic and cultural treasures, and possesses an individual charm: buildings everywhere are of pleasing architectural form and proportional harmony, with close attention to ornamental detail. It lies proudly along the banks of the River Vltava, amid the gentle surroundings of the hills which characterise this part of Bohemia. Prague has been a melting-pot of ethnic groups since ancient times, existing by combining Czech elements with Jewish and German ones, and allowing the development of religious movements, trade and commerce, and of industry, thanks to its favourable geographic position on the communication routes between Central and Eastern Europe, and between the North and South of the vast German and Slavonic area. Modern Prague shrewdly eyes the tourist armed with Dollars and Marks; a jealous keeper of its mysteries, the city is reluctant to reveal itself to the curiosity of those wanting to unearth the secrets of the alchemists of the past. The birthplace or one-time residence of many famous people, such as the astronomers Tycho Brahe and Johannes Kepler, the Dientzenhofers, Albert Einstein, Wolfgang Amadeus Mozart, Antonín Dvořák, Bedřich Smetana, Jaroslav Hašek, Franz Kafka, Charles IV, Jan Hus, St John Nepomuk, and many other illustrious figures, the city bears witness to cultures and civilisations from all over the world. Over the centuries it has survived wars and disasters, and not even the tanks of the Warsaw Pact were able to defeat its rebellious nature: the people's and the nation's thirst for freedom was satisfied 23 years after Jan Palach had been engulfed by flames, making him the martyr of a shattered "Spring".

Bohemian coats of arms.

The first settlements on the site of the modern city date back to Neolithic times, and fortified settlements were first recorded in the 9th century. Primitive centres joined together around the fortresses of Hradčany and Vyšehrad between the 9th and 10th centuries, and from that time onwards the Přemyslids made this the most important castle in Bohemia. As a result it became the focal point for the activities of craftsmen and merchants, attracting mainly Jews and Germans. Having become a Bishop's See in 973, Prague obtained city status between 1232 and 1235. Charles IV then made it the capital of the Empire, founding the University here in 1348 and preparing the ground for large scale urban development. In 1419 the followers of Želivský freed the Hussites held prisoner in the New Town Hall, and threw out the Catholic counsellors. This marked the beginning of a long period of religious conflict. In fact, the ascension of the Habsburgs in 1526 marked the decline of Prague, and this became even more marked after the failure of the revolt

Habsburg eagle.

against the Viennese sovereigns in 1547. While having suffered limitations to its autonomy and the loss of its Court, which had been transferred to Vienna, the city underwent a brief period of revival under Rudolph II who settled here between 1583-1610, and who also contributed to the Germanisation of the city. The Czech revolt of 1618, which began with the "Second Prague Defenestration", led to the Thirty Years' War. Following its defeat in the Battle of the White Mountain (8th Nov 1620) Prague entered a period of deep decline from all points of view: the wave of middle-class emigration in the first half of the 17th century was of biblical proportions. The uprisings of 1848 failed in their attempt to gain freedom for the Slavs who opposed the centralisation policy introduced by Joseph II. 1861 marked a clear turning-point with the success of the Slavs in the municipal elections. Between the 19th and 20th centuries the economic and industrial development of Prague led to a considerable influx of the rural population, and caused a growing interest on the part of the nobility in cultural and intellectual pursuits. After the First World War Prague was proclaimed the Capital of Czechoslovakia. The city endured the brutal domination of the Nazis from 1939 until 1945 when it was liberated by the Russians and the Americans. In 1948 a Communist coup d'état transformed Czechoslovakia into a Popular Republic, and 1960 marked the birth of the Czechoslovakian Socialist Republic. The long ordeal seemed to be coming to an end in 1968 when the new, more liberal programme adopted by Dubček (the so-called "Prague Spring"), appeared to open the way towards reform and civil liberties. However, the ever-present threat of the Soviet, Communist monolith was brutally felt on 20th August 1968 when tanks were sent into Prague, causing the indignant reaction of its inhabitants, and culminating in the suicides of the students Palach and Zajic. Twenty years later a protest march was held against the Soviet occupiers to demand liberty and civil rights. Despite police repression, which was repeated a year later to oppose the demands of the "Charta 77" movement, this event later led, through the "Velvet Revolution", to the fall of

the Communist Regime in Czechoslovakia and to the resignation of Gustav Husák. Václav Havel took his place and became President of the Republic at the end of 1989. The free elections of 1990 marked the victory of the list led by Havel and Dubček, the latter having returned to his country after his exile. On 1st January 1993 the division of the Federal Republic of Czechoslovakia was ratified, giving rise to the Czech and the Slovak Republics, with Prague and Bratislava as their respective capitals.

WELCOME TO PRAGUE, TOUR OF THE CITY

Approaching the city from the air, over the sharp bends of the Vltava, the majestic and austere beauty of Prague appears with the bell towers, spires and buildings which have given it the deserved title of "Paris of the East". The city stands out like a precious stone set in the green surroundings of the gentle hills of Bohemia.
But once one has landed in the modern, functional **Ruzyně Airport** and arrived in the city after a transfer of about 20km, there is no more time for reflection. What remains instead is the difficult task of choosing between the many attractions on offer in "The Golden City". Prague is undoubtedly a fascinating city, although rich in striking contrasts: the central areas are those subjected to the incessant pressure of tourists, from the inevitable

View of Prague from Petřín Observation Tower.

Japanese, the tireless Germans, the innumerable Spanish and English, to the Italians, as noisy and easily identifiable as ever. These quarters make it easy to see why Prague is often compared to Vienna, Paris or London, thanks to the elegant shops and nightclubs, first-class restaurants and hotels, the tidy, clean streets, and the punctual and efficient public transport system (even though both its visual and spoken indications are all in Czech). In this melting pot of languages, cultures and nationalities Prague has what it takes to compete with the ability and confidence of the most advanced Central European and Western metropolises. However, in the quarters just outside the centre and in the suburbs, despite the fact that the buildings are still well looked-after and the streets orderly and clean, the gap which separates the Czech standard of living from that of nearby Austria and Germany is clearly visible. Fifty years of Communism have left their mark on the country's economy and the consequences are easy to see. The city is one huge building site, work going on continuously in order to make up for lost time, and to keep up with its European counterparts.

A tour round the quarters of Prague might begin at the citadel of **Hradčany** with its Castle, its monumental buildings, the Loreto shrine and the Strahov Monastery. This is one of the highest quarters in Prague and the views it offers over Malá Strana and Staré Město are some of the most charming and eloquent in the city.

Descending from the Castle, beyond the *Nerudova*, lies the picturesque quarter of **Malá Strana**. Here we find various austere buildings (mainly the home to embassies), imposing Baroque churches, and an important attraction for the faithful, the "Holy Infant of Prague", kept in the Church of Our Lady Victorious. The wooded hill of Petřín, with its numerous attractions, is one of the capital's greenest areas. Characteristic of this quarter are the ever-present craft workshops and the "vinárny" with their attractive and imaginative signs.

Beyond Charles Bridge, with its emblematic statues, throngs of tourists, jugglers and vendors, lies **Staré Město**, the "Old Town", with its magical, alluring atmosphere and its treasures of art, history and architecture. The narrow streets, bursting with people and lined with shops selling sou-

Kříž House (Old Town Hall), detail of the façade.

View of Vyšehrad.

venirs and local products, lead invariably to the architectural jewel of *Staroměstské náměstí*, a theatrical composition of buildings, churches and monuments in an incredible hubbub of tourists, horse-drawn carriages and orderly market stalls.

To the north of this square, one of Prague's main attractions, lies the **Josefov** quarter. This is the Jewish area, one of the most charming parts of the capital, with its Ghetto, Jewish museum, synagogues, cemetery and the ancient memories of a people and culture which survived centuries of persecution.

Wandering from *Staroměstské náměstí* towards the "Golden Cross" (the crossroads where the quarter's main thoroughfares meet), it is surprising to note the meticulous care and attention given to the ornamental detail of the buildings: splendid attics, tympanums, statues, stuccowork, friezes and various other decorations enrich and refine the buildings' façades, transforming even an anonymous building into a small architectural masterpiece.

We are now in *Na Příkopě,* near *Wenceslas Square*, the fulcrum and heart of modern Prague. Further south lies **Nové Město**, the "New Town", with its imposing Town Hall and enormous square named after King Charles. Majestic buildings, interesting churches and the legend of Dr Faust are all within the visitor's reach.

Last, but by no means least, the **Vyšherad** quarter is an obligatory stop for those wishing to really get to know the city. It is easily reached by underground, and not far from the station are some of the most recent architectural achievements in Prague's urban history (the Forum Hotel and the Palace of Culture). These exist side by side with one of the oldest settlements on the banks of the Vltava. Vyšherad is not only a quarter; not only does it bear important witness to the history and art, past and present, of this extraordinary city, but it is also, and above all a serene oasis of peace, a tranquil area of greenery a little off the beaten tourist track, and it is perhaps precisely for this reason that it possesses such quiet beauty and affords such enchanting views over the Vltava, the hills and the city itself.

THE CASTLE AREA

THE CASTLE - HRADČANSKÉ NÁMĚSTÍ - NATIONAL GALLERY COLLECTION OF EUROPEAN ART - SCHWARZENBERG PALACE - MUSEUM OF MILITARY HISTORY - ARCHBISHOP'S PALACE - MARTINITZ PALACE - WALLENSTEIN PALACE - BELVEDERE - LETENSKÉ SADY

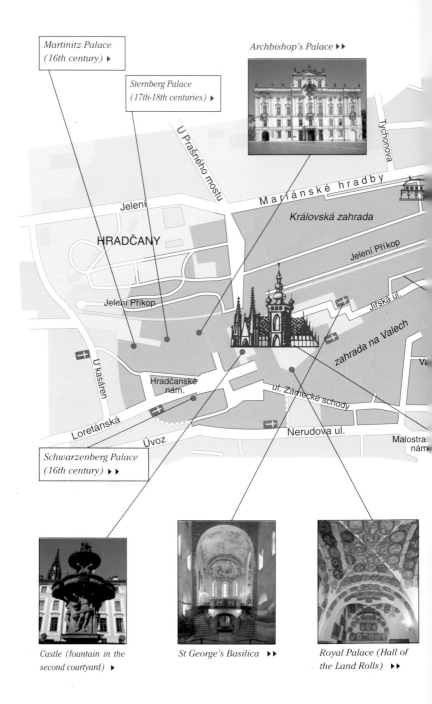

Martinitz Palace
(16th century) ▸

Archbishop's Palace ▸▸

Sternberg Palace
(17th-18th centuries) ▸

Schwarzenberg Palace
(16th century) ▸▸

Castle (fountain in the
second courtyard) ▸

St George's Basilica ▸▸

Royal Palace (Hall of
the Land Rolls) ▸▸

8

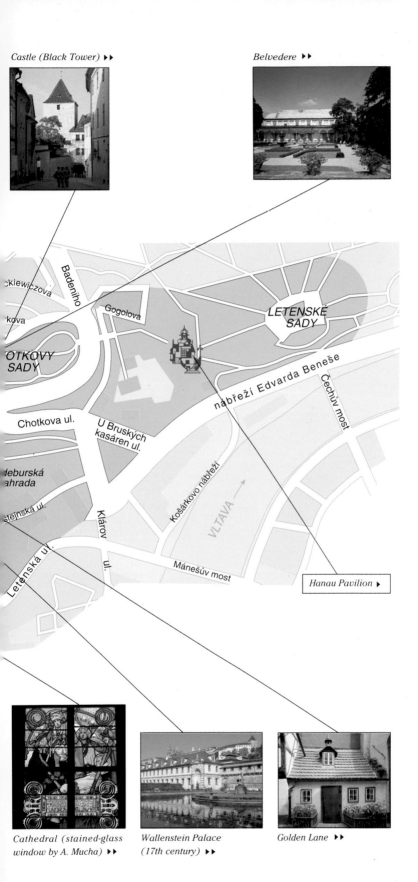

Castle (Black Tower) ▶▶

Belvedere ▶▶

Badeniho

:kiewiczova

kova

Gogolova

LETENSKÉ
SADY

OTKOVY
SADY

nábřeží Edvarda Beneše

Čechův most

Chotkova ul.

U Bruských
kasáren ul.

deburská
ahrada

Košářkovo nábřeží

VLTAVA →

stejnská ul.

Klárov

ul.

Máneśův most

Letenská ul.

Hanau Pavilion ▶

Cathedral (stained-glass
window by A. Mucha) ▶▶

Wallenstein Palace
(17th century) ▶▶

Golden Lane ▶▶

The Castle viewed from the Vltava.

The Castle (*Hradčany*) - One of the largest fortresses in the world, the Castle of Prague represents the essence of the Bohemian city and the historical memory of the infant Czech Republic. It was founded by the Přemyslids in the second half of the 9th century, and the additions made over the centuries, following episodes of fire and devastation, give us the grand complex as we see it today. It is a combination of Romanesque, Gothic, Renaissance and Baroque elements which bear witness to the stratification of various cultures, historical eras, architectural and artistic trends. The **Grand Courtyard** (also called the First Courtyard) was com-

Hradčanské náměstí, Castle entrance.

'Fighting Giants', detail of the Castle entrance gate.

pleted in the Habsburg period (18th century); Maria Theresa of Austria entrusted the project to the Court architect, N. Pacassi, and the work was carried out under the direction of A. Lurago. On the piers of the entrance gate are copies of I. Platzer the Elder's *Fighting Giants* (18th century). The **Second Courtyard** is reached through the 17th century **Matthias Gate** and is decorated with a 17th century Baroque fountain with sculptures by H. Kohl. The *Fountain of Lions* was added in the late 1960s. The building in the north-western corner of the courtyard has housed the **Castle Gallery** (*Hradní galerie*) since 1965, and this includes paintings previously displayed in the Rudolph and Ferdinand II galleries. This interesting gallery contains works by excellent Czechoslovakian and European artists. Among the most important are Jacopo Robusti, known as 'Tintoretto' (*Shepherds in Adoration of Jesus, Jesus and the Adulterer*); Titian (*Young*

Chapel of the Holy Rood.

Evening view of the Cathedral.

Woman, better known as *The Toilet of a Young Lady*); P. Brandl (*Paul the Apostle*); Veronese (*Saint Catherine with the Angel*); G. Reni (*Nessus and Deianeira*); P.P. Rubens (*The Assembly of the Olympic Gods*); Hans von Aachen (*Portrait of the Emperor Matthias*); Jan Kupecky; J.P. Brandl. The sculptures by M. Braun and A. de Vries are also worthy of note. Some of these artists were only identified for certain in the 1960s.

On the opposite side of the courtyard is the **Chapel of the Holy Rood**, built by A. Lurago in the 18th century; it houses the Treasury of St Vitus's Cathedral which, since 1961, has contained the Treasure of St Vitus including sacred ornaments and vestments, and various jewels. The walls bear paintings by V. Kandler and J. Navratil, while the sculptures from the same era are by E. Max (*St Peter and St Paul, St John Nepomuk*). The **Third Courtyard**, once the hub of fortress activity, contains the central nucleus of the Castle - the Cathedral, the Old Provost's Lodging and the Royal Palace.

St Vitus's Cathedral (*Chrám svatého Víta*) - The history of this majestic edifice, only completed in 1929, begins around 926 when St Wenceslas had the rotunda of St Vitus built on the same site. More than a century later a Romanesque basilica rose here, and on these foundations a Gothic cathedral was later erected, starting in the first half of the 14th century. The plans were drawn up by M. D'Arras, a French architect invited to Prague by Charles IV. He started the eastern side, taking inspiration from early French Gothic and using the cathedrals of Toulouse and Narbonne as models. The work he began included the Cathedral chancel which is particularly impressive in size, being 47m long and 39m high. On the death of D'Arras the work was taken over by Peter Parler (1359) who enriched the Cathedral, modelling it on German Gothic style. His sons, Jan and Václav, subsequently took over and continued work on the building from 1399 until 1420, completing the Chancel and beginning the base of the highest of the towers, the mighty steeple. This impressive bell tower stands 99m tall, dominating the Cathedral; in the latter half of the 16th century Hans of Tyrol and B. Wohlmüt added its Renaissance steeple and balustrade, while the uppermost pinnacle in Baroque style was added by Pacassi (1770). The bell tower houses the 16th century *St Sigismund bell* which is the largest in Bohemia. In 1872 J. Mocker started work to complete the grandiose building. He adhered faithfully to the plans drawn up by Peter Parler, working on the western part of the cathedral which is notable for its fine neo-Gothic features. The main portal was also begun at that time, and completed in 1929 by K. Hilbert. The cathedral, now finally completed, was consecrated in the same year, 1000 years after the death of St Wenceslas. The beautiful **façade**, wedged in between twin steeples, is a masterpiece of neo-Gothic architecture, and is remarkable for its ornate decoration, particularly in the central rose window and the portals. This decorative work was carried out during the completion stage, between the second half of the 19th century and the first half of the 20th century. The fine rose window, showing *Scenes from the Creation,* was created by F. Kysela between 1925 and 1927. The monumental **interior**, a triumph of Gothic, is incredibly vast: it is 124m long and 33m high in the main nave, and 60m wide across the transept. This is the largest church in Prague and one of the most majestic buildings in the entire Castle complex. The interior is divided into three naves by massive pillars supporting ogival arches. Note the beautiful ribbed cross-vaults, and the magnificent finely illustrated mosaic windows. Some of these windows are the remarkable work of 20th century Czech artists; note for example the window crafted by A. Mucha (third chapel of the left-hand nave). The triforium holds the busts of the Cathedral's designers, illustrious figures, and members of Charles IV's family. The southern portal (or *Golden Portal*) is crowned on the outside by a 14th century mosaic (*Last Judgement*), and decorated with the portraits of *Charles IV* and *Elizabeth of Pomerania*. Higher still is the mullioned window showing the *Last Judgement*. This was designed in 1934 by M. Švabinský who used no fewer than 40,000 pieces of glass. In the chancel situated opposite there is a majestic 18th century organ. The *Imperial Tomb*, in front of the high altar, is a kind of Habsburg mausoleum; it was completed in the second half of the 16th century by A Colijn and is decorated with the statues of *Ferdinand I*, *Anne*, and *Maximilian II*. Members of the royal family are portrayed in the medallions. The chapel of *St Wenceslas* is one of the most interesting of the many chapels: it was built in the 14th century by P. Parler on the site of the earlier rotunda which contained the remains of St Wenceslas. Observe the beautiful decoration in semi-precious Bohemian stones. The frescoes of the *Passion* were

Cathedral, detail of the rose window viewed from inside.

painted by Master Oswald of Prague in the 14th century; those depicting the *Legend of St Wenceslas* date from the 16th century and are by the Master of the Litoměřice Altar. The chapel leads to the *Royal Treasury* (containing the Bohemian crown jewels, and only open at certain times). The nearby *Chapel of the Holy Rood*, decorated with a fourteenth century painting (*The Vernicle*), leads down to the *Royal Crypt.* This was renovated in the first half of the 20th century and contains the remains of the Bohemian sovereigns (including Charles IV, Wenceslas IV, Ladislav Postumus, Jiří of Poděbrady and Rudolph II). The *Old Sacristy,* otherwise known as *St Michael's Chapel*, is noted for its fine stellar vaulting, the work of P. Parler. Close to *St Anne's Chapel* is a delicately carved wooden panel depicting *The Flight of Frederick V of the Palatinate;* this refers to a famous episode in the city's history, The Battle of the White Mountain in 1620. The most interesting feature of this carving is, however, a minute and richly detailed image of Prague as it was in 1630. The choir chapel dedicated to *St John Nepomuk* is of particular interest for its silver busts of *St Adalbert, St Cyril, St Wenceslas* and *St Vitus* (late 17th century). In front of this is the elaborate *Tomb of St John Nepomuk*, crafted in silver by A. Corradini and J.J. Würth in the first half of the 18th century, following a design by J.E. Fischer von Erlach. In the centre of the apse, behind the high altar, is the *Lady Chapel*. This contains several tombs by artists from the Parler workshop. In front of the chapel is the *Tomb of St Vitus*, and the statue representing the Cathedral's saint is by J. Max. The adjacent *Chapel of the Holy Relics*, also known as the *Saxon Chapel,* contains the tombs of the Přemyslids, from the Parler workshop.

Cathedral, Chapel of St Wenceslas.

Cathedral, Tomb of St John Nepomuk.

Nocturnal view of the Castle from the Vltava.

Partial view of the Royal Palace.

Old Provost's Lodging (*Staré proboštství*) - Once the Bishop's Palace, this building flanks the façade and southern side of the Cathedral. It was restored in Baroque style in the 1600s. Note the 17th century *Statue of St Wenceslas* by J.J. Bendl. Near the building stands the granite *Obelisk* (1928), erected to commemorate those who died in the First World War, and the *Equestrian Statue of St George* (a copy of the 14th century original by Georg and Martin von Klausenburg).

Royal Palace (*Královský palác*) - The palace was built in the 11th century on the site of a 9th century prince's court. It was originally Romanesque in style, but subsequently rebuilt and extended (in the 12th, 13th, 14th and 15th centuries). It was the seat of the Bohemian sovereigns up until the Habsburg period. One of the most important of the palace's many rooms is the *Vladislav Hall*, designed by B. Rieth of Piesting and built between the 15th and 16th centuries. Observe in particular the magnificent Gothic rib

Royal Palace, Vladislav Hall.

Royal Palace, Riders' Staircase.

vaulting. Once used for royal coronations, the hall is now the setting for the election of the President of the Republic. The adjoining *All Saints' Chapel* was built in the 14th century by P. Parler and was later remodelled and enlarged after a fire in the latter half of the 16th century. A painting of the

Royal Palace, Bohemian Chancellery.   *Royal Palace, All Saints' Chapel.*

17

The façade of St George's Basilica.

All Saints decorates the high altar which dates from the mid 18th century. On the right hand side altar there is a late Renaissance *Deposition. The Diet Hall*, built in the 16th century, was reconstructed following a fire in the second half of the same century. It is here that the President of the Republic is today sworn in, and where, on particular occasions, the Czech National Council meets. Lastly, it is worth visiting the *Louis Palace* with its *Bohemian Chancellery* (which houses a copy by Velázquez of a *Portrait of Philip IV,* and which was the scene of the "defenestration" of the imperial governors which marked the prelude to the Thirty Years' War), and the *Green Chamber*, decorated with numerous coats of arms and once the setting for royal audiences and administration of justice.

St George's Basilica (*Bazilika svatého Jiří*) - This Romanesque building with its 17th century Baroque **façade** opens onto the *Jiřské náměstí*, opposite the Cathedral apse. The basilica is one of the best examples of Romanesque architecture in Bohemia. Dominated by twin towers, it was founded by Prince Vratislav between 915 and 921 and has been rebuilt several times following various episodes of destruction. The central nave is distinguished by its architectural features dating back to between the 10th and 12th centuries. Traces of some 13th century frescoes (*Heavenly Jerusalem*) can be seen on the ceiling of the chancel, while the ceiling of the apse is decorated with frescoes showing *The Coronation of Our Lady*. The *Crypt* (mid-12th century) houses a *Statue of St Bridget* by B. Spinetti. The *Chapel of St John Nepomuk* was added in the 18th century. Note the *Statue* of the saint on the façade, and the ceiling frescoes (*Apotheosis of St John Nepomuk*). The 13th century *Chapel of St Ludmilla* contains the *Sepulchre* of the saint, patron of Bohemia, by P. Parler (14th century). Some 19th century frescoes by J.V. Hellich depict *Events from the Life of St Ludmilla*, and other late 16th century religious paintings can also be seen.

National Gallery Collection of Early Bohemian Art (*Sbírka starého českého umění Národní galerie*) - These important collections are exhibited in the adjacent **St George's Convent,** a Benedictine building constructed in 973, and destroyed, rebuilt and transformed several times. It was the first building to be founded by this monastic order in Bohemia. The Baroque reconstruction work was carried out in the latter half of the 17th century. The monastery ceased to function as such in the latter half of the 18th century, and between 1962 and 1974 it was renovated in order

A detail of the interior of St George's Basilica.

to house the art collections. These begin, in chronological order, with the Gothic works whose subject is mainly the Virgin Mary, and which were brought here from churches around Bohemia. As well as some early Gothic sculptures of *Madonnas*, the northern corridor (on the lower floor) contains the magnificent tympanum from the Church of Our Lady of the Snows. The 13th century *Cycle of the Master of the Vyšší Brod Altar* is inspired by episodes from the life of Christ. The *Statue of St George on Horseback*, at one time situated in the third courtyard of the Castle, was sculpted in the 14th century by Martin and Georg von Klausenburg. The *Master Theoderick Hall* contains some of the panel paintings by this out-standing artist of the "beautiful style" of Gothic painting in Bohemia (14th century), commissioned by Charles IV. On the ground floor, one of the halls contains the *Cycle of the Master Of Třeboň*, with fragments of altar pieces showing themes from the life of Christ, images of saints and apos-tles. Another hall contains the tympanum of the northern portal of the Church of Our Lady of Týn, the work of artists from the Parler workshop (15th century). The northern corridor contains numerous paintings and sculptures inspired by the Madonna (14th - 15th centuries), and a 15th cen-tury *Crucifixion* by the Master of Raigern. The Renaissance is represented by the *Lamentation of Christ* by Žebrák, *The Visitation of the Virgin Mary* by the Master of the Litoměřice Altar, and the wooden reliquary by the Master IP, a follower of A. Dürer. On the first floor are exhibits of works by the Mannerists active at the Bohemian court (H. von Aachen, B. Spranger,

19

View of the Golden Lane.

J.H. Roelandt Savery, A. de Vries); works by Baroque painters and sculptors (J.P. Brandl, V.V. Reiner, J. Kupecký, M.L. Willmann, I.F. Platzer, F.M. Brokoff, M.B. Braun); and works by Rococo painters (A. Kern, N. Grund).

Golden Lane (*Zlatá ulička*) - This picturesque little street is an essential stop for visitors to the Castle. Also known as the *Alchemists' Lane,* it is evidence of "The Magical City", for it is here in the laboratories of the Mihulka Tower that Rudolph II's alchemists are supposed to have pursued the myths of the philosophers' stone and the production of gold. At least, this is how the legend goes, and it is certainly one of the most charming to have flourished around "The Golden City". However, it would appear that in reality these little cottages were built towards the end of the 16th century to house Rudolph II's guards. Only later did the goldsmiths establish themselves here. Today, various shops attract the tourists: the cottages which were once home to craftsmen and the city's poor are now picturesque little stores selling souvenirs and local arts and crafts. At n° 22 between 1912 and 1914 Kafka wrote some of his stories, and the poet

Inside Lobkowitz Palace.

The Castle square (Hradčanské náměstí).

Jaroslav Seifert, who won the Nobel prize in 1984, also lived in this charming corner of the Czech capital for a while.

Not far from here, in the southern wing of the Castle, is **Lobkowitz Palace**, once the Burgrave's Residence, and today the "House of Czech Children". Within the palace there is an exhibition of the history of Bohemia, which extends from the Roman period to the mid-19th century.

Hradčanské náměstí - This charming square, given a certain dignity by the Baroque buildings which overlook it, has always formed the entrance to the Castle. It is adorned with the 18th century **Plague Column** (F.M. Brokoff). The surrounding buildings are the result of the reconstruction work carried out after the fire of 1541.

National Gallery Collection of European Art (*Sbírka evropského umení Národní galerie*) - Since 1949 this collection has been on show in the Baroque **Sternberg Palace** (17th-18th centuries) and includes works by Italian, German, Dutch, French and other European artists. The palace takes its name from Franz Josef Sternberg who founded the "Society of Patriotic Friends of the Arts" in 1796. The works of art made available by its members gradually increased in number and, before the Second World War, the collection became the property of the State. Paintings by 14th and 15th century Italian artists are displayed on the first floor, including Sebastiano del Piombo, Antonio Vivarini, Palma the Elder, and Piero della Francesca. We then find 15th and 16th century Dutch artists such as P. Brueghel the Elder (*Haymaking*); P. Brueghel the Younger (*Winter Landscape*); G. tot Sint Jans; J. Gossaert (*St Luke Drawing the Virgin*). On the second floor are paintings by 16th - 18th century Italian artists such as Canaletto (*View of London*); Veronese, Palma the Younger, Tintoretto (*David with Goliath's Head*); Tiepolo (*Portrait of Venetian Patrician*). Other noteworthy Italian painters of the same period are G. Reni and Agnolo di Cosimo, known as "Il Bronzino". Next come the artists from the German school, most importantly A. Dürer (*The Feast of the Rosary*). Others worthy of note are H. Holbein the Elder, H. Baldung Grien, L. Cranach the Elder (*Adam and Eve*), and Altdorfer. The most outstanding among the Flemish and Dutch 17th century artists are P.P. Rubens (*Cleopatra, St Augustine, Martyrdom of St Thomas*); A. van Dyck (*Abraham and Isaac*); F. Hals (*Portrait of Gaspar Schode*); J. Jordaens (*Apostles*); Rembrandt (*Rabbi*). Spanish 16th century painting is represented by a canvas by El

The mock rustication on Schwarzenberg Palace.

Greco (D. Theotokópulos) depicting the *Head of Christ*. Two floors of the northern and western wings house the works of the 19th and 20th century Masters: G. Klimt, O. Kokoschka (noted for his views of Prague, including the famous *Charles Bridge and Hradčany*), C.D. Friedrich, R. Guttuso, G. Manzù, Delacroix, Courbet, Monet, Cézanne, Gauguin, Renoir, Van Gogh, Toulouse-Lautrec, Matisse, Picasso and Chagall.

Schwarzenberg Palace - Museum of Military History (*Schwarzenberský palác - Vojenské muzeum*) - The building as it is today is in fine Renaissance style, clearly imitating northern Italian prototypes. Its designer, the Italian architect A. Galli, commissioned by the Lobkowitz family, carried out the work between 1545 and 1576. Observe how the external decoration, made with the *sgraffito* technique, looks exactly as if the masonry is clad in projecting pyramid shaped stones. The beautiful exterior decoration dates from the 16th century but was renovated between the 19th and 20th centuries. The Museum of Military History collections have

The architectural elegance of the Archbishop's Palace.

been housed in the 16th century wing of the palace since 1945 and are enclosed in rooms of elaborate decoration. They include prehistoric weapons, arms supplied to the various European armies up until 1918, cannons, uniforms, medals, flags, military maps and plans of famous battles.

Archbishop's Palace (*Arcibiskupsky palác*) - The original building was a Renaissance residence which was then transformed in the second half of the 16th century, extended around 1600 and converted to Baroque style in the second half of the 17th century. In the same period the architect J.B. Mathey, who had designed the Baroque transformations, completed the splendid main portal. In the second half of the 18th century J.J. Wirch gave the palace's **façade** its present day Rococo appearance. Above the coat of arms of the Prince-Archbishop A.P. Příchovský there is a group of sculpted figures by I.F. Platzer. The exquisite interior furnishings in late-Baroque style are also the work of Wirch. Note in particular the nine gobelins, the wood carvings, the stucco decorations and the collections of porcelain and crystal. Ferdinand I bought the palace in 1562 for the Archbishop who had just returned to Prague at the end of the Hussite wars. It is still the Bishop's See today.

Martinitz Palace (*Martinický palác*) - The origins of this Renaissance building date back to the 16th century. In the first half of the 17th century it was bought by Jaroslav Bořita of Martinitz (the protagonist of the second "Prague defenestration"), who had the palace extended and decorated. Note the Renaissance *sgraffiti* (*Episodes from the Life of Hercules*), which decorate the eastern side. Similar decorations, with biblical themes, were brought to light on the side which faces the square during restoration work in the early 1970s, thus making it possible to once again admire the beautiful 16th century façade.

Wallenstein Palace (*Valdštejnský palác*) - This magnificent residence, somewhere between a palace and a fortress, was built in the first half of the 17th century for the Bohemian commander Albrecht Wenzel Eusebius von Wallenstein. The plans were drawn up by A. Spezza and G. Pironi and the work carried out by G.B. Marini. The building is a clear example of a residence commissioned by a layman, in direct antagonism with the regal power. Wallenstein wanted his actions and grandeur to be reflected in the majestic palace, and this self-congratulatory intention is clear from the paintings which portray him. The ceiling of the *Hall of Cavaliers* bears a 17th century fresco (*Wallenstein in the Guise of Mars in his Triumphal Chariot*). The other rooms are decorated with paintings, including a *Portrait of Wallenstein on Horseback*. The palace chapel's altar is said to be the oldest in the city. The building is also the seat of the Ministry of Culture and houses the **J. Á. Komenský (Comenius) Museum** with exhibits on this 16th-17th century humanist. The **Wallenstein Garden**

Grandiose perspective of Wallenstein Palace.

(*Valdštejnská zahrada*) is also a part of the palace complex. It was modelled on the prototype of the Italian Baroque garden, and contains copies of sculptures by A. de Vries. The *Sala Terrena* (Garden Pavilion), with frescoes by B. del Bianco, is used for theatrical and concert performances.

Belvedere (*Královský letohrádek*) - This palace was the summer residence which Ferdinand I had built for his wife, Anne. It was constructed in the 16th century, at the same time as the royal garden. Its design, with its prominent Renaissance features, was drawn up by P. della Stella. The frieze above the portals on the ground floor bears an ornamental motive showing themes inspired by Greek mythology. The ornamentation is completed with sculptures of gods (18th century) and a *Portrait of Ferdinand I.* Inside, the hall was painted with frescoes in the 19th century by C. Ruben. The famous astronomer, Tycho Brahe, stayed at the Summer Palace for a short time. Nearby is the *Singing Fountain* (1568), a work in bronze by T. Jaroš. Its curious name derives from the melody produced by the water as it hits the basin.

Letenské sady - From the grassy hillside of Letná (or the "summer hill"), which slopes down to the Vltava, there is a well-known view over the city, from the Castle to the Cathedral, and as far as Petřín hill. Situated in this area is the **Hanau Pavilion**, set up for the 1891 Exhibition and later converted to a panoramic restaurant; the **Praha Expo 58,** the Czechoslovakian pavilion at the Brussels Expo '58 which was afterwards transported to the hillside and turned into a restaurant; **Sparta ČKD's Stadium,** enlarged at the end of the 1960s to a capacity of 40,000; and other sports grounds and facilities.

Belvedere, Singing Fountain.

THE MALÁ STRANA ('LITTLE QUARTER') AREA

NERUDOVA ULICE - MORZIN PALACE - THUN-HOHENSTEIN PALACE - CHURCH OF ST THOMAS - **MALÁ STRANA** - MALOSTRANSKÉ NÁMĚSTÍ - VRTBA PALACE - **CHURCH OF ST NICHOLAS IN MALÁ STRANA** - NOSTITZ PALACE - GRAND PRIORY OF THE KNIGHTS OF MALTA - BUQUOY PALACE

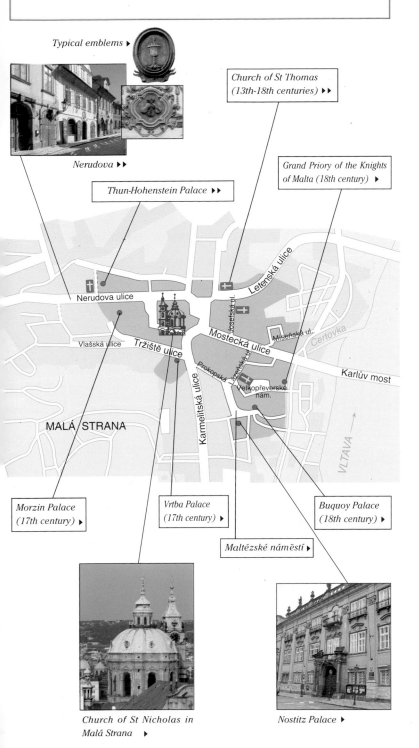

Typical emblems ▶

Nerudova ▶▶

Church of St Thomas (13th-18th centuries) ▶▶

Grand Priory of the Knights of Malta (18th century) ▶

Thun-Hohenstein Palace ▶▶

Nerudova ulice

Letenská ulice

Josefská pl.

Mostecká ulice

Miseňská ul.

Certovka

Karlův most

Vlašská ulice

Tržíště ulice

Karmelitská ulice

Prokopská

Lázenská pl.

Lázenská pl.

Velkopřevorské nám.

MALÁ STRANA

VLTAVA

Morzin Palace (17th century) ▶

Vrtba Palace (17th century) ▶

Buquoy Palace (18th century) ▶

Maltézské náměstí ▶

Church of St Nicholas in Malá Strana ▶

Nostitz Palace ▶

Thun-Hohenstein Palace,
seat of the Italian Embassy.

Nerudova ulice - This street, which branches off from *Malostranské náměstí* and climbs steeply up to the Castle, is one of the most characteristic and charming corners of the Malá Strana quarter. One of its main features is its wealth of elegant houses, some of the finest examples of late Baroque building in Prague. Characteristic coats of arms and shop signs, and picturesque front doors capture the visitor's attention: n° 12 was the home of the lute-makers, the Edlingers, and the sign with three crossed violins is still here today; **Valkoun House**, at n° 14 was remodelled in late Baroque style by G. Santini; typical signs can also be seen on the houses named **The Golden Cup** (N° 16, Renaissance style), and **St John Nepomuk** (n° 18, Baroque); the **Theatine Monastery** (n° 24) was the setting for performances of the *Kajetan Dramas* in Czech, while the adjacent building, **The Rocking Donkey**, supplied the setting for a story by Neruda; n° 32 is the quarter's old pharmacy, restored in 1980 and now housing the **Museum of Pharmacy in Countries of the Bohemian Crown;** n° 33 is the **Bretfeld Palace**, also known as *Summer and Winter*; it was here that famous people such as Casanova and Mozart stayed; on the front door of the **House at the Golden Horseshoe** (n° 34) there is an image of *St Wenceslas*; at n° 49 a white swan forms the sign of an elegant Baroque residence. A nearby flight of steps leads to the Castle.

Morzin Palace (*Morzinský palác*) - This building, which houses the Rumanian Embassy, is at n° 5 *Nerudova ulice*. It is the result of the joining together of three buildings, carried out in the second half of the 17th century, and is considered to be one of the finest examples of Baroque architecture in Malá Strana. Václav Morzin had the building transformed in the first half of the 18th century. The early Baroque details are still visible (on the side wings), while the Baroque interventions by G. Santini and the sculptures by F.M. Brokoff blend together in an attractive equilibrium. Note the allegories of *Day and Night* above the portal, and the *Moors* supporting the balcony.

Thun-Hohenstein Palace (*Thun-Hohenštejnský palác*) - Situated at n° 20 *Nerudova ulice*, the palace is home to the **Italian Embassy**. A handsome building with elegant Baroque forms, it was built in the first half of the 18th century. The plans were drawn up by G. Santini who was commissioned by N.V. Kolovrat. Observe the magnificent portal, crowned with two *Eagles with Outstretched Wings*, the Kolovrats' heraldic emblem. Higher still are the statues of *Jupiter* and *Juno*.

View of the interior of the Church of St Thomas.

Church of St Thomas (*Kostel svatého Tomáše*) - This Augustinian building preserves clear traces of its early Gothic origins, despite the Baroque restoration work carried out by K.I Dientzenhofer in the first half of the 18th century. The church was founded by Wenceslas II in 1285 as a place of worship for the Augustinians, and was completed a century later. The **façade** is adorned with a Renaissance portal by Campione dei Bossi (17th century), and statues of *St Augustine* and *St Thomas*, the late 17th century work of H. Kohl. The **interior** is remarkable for its magnificent decoration by Bohemian artists who produced a wealth of paintings and sculptures here. The ceiling frescoes (*Episodes from the Life of St Augustine*) were painted by V.V. Reiner in the 18th century, and the paintings in the dome and chancel (*The Legend of St Thomas*) are also attributed to him. The 18th century high altar is by K. Kovář and it is embellished with sculptures of *Saints* by I. Müller, J.A. Quittainer, and F.M. Brokoff. 17th century works by Škréta adorn the transept altar (*St Thomas*) and the chancel (*Assumption of the Virgin*). Rudolph's court architect, O. Aostalli, and the sculptor A. de Vries are buried in the church.

Malá Strana (*Little Quarter*) - The quarter of Malà Strana grew up, starting in 1257, on the left bank of the Vltava, between the hills of Hradčany and Petřín. It was founded by Přemysl Otakar II whose intention it was to create a home for the German colonists. At the time of Charles IV the urban network underwent considerable expansion: old churches were restored or completed, and fortifications and defensive works appeared everywhere. During the 15th and 16th centuries the quarter was tormented by fires, as a result of which the building and extension work intensified, transforming Malá Strana into a coveted residential quarter. The area was chosen by the nobility and the wealthy as their permanent residence, and they enriched it with sumptuous palaces and magnificent churches. Malá Strana's charm was enhanced by the fact that the coronation processions of the Bohemian sovereigns passed through its very streets.

Malostranské náměstí - The ancient heart of the Malá Strana quarter centres around two small squares, both surrounded by buildings of considerable architectural importance. The upper square contains the 17th century **Plague Column**, with sculptures reproducing the *Holy Trinity* and the *Patron Saints of Bohemia* by F. Geiger and J.O. Mayer. Both squares were previously decorated with fountains: the upper one was replaced by the Plague Column, and the lower one by a *Monument to Radetzky* (today kept

View over the rooftops of Malá Strana towards Staré Město.

in the Lapidarium of the National Museum). The most noteworthy buildings are **Kaiserštejn Palace**, created in the first half of the 17th century by joining together pre-existing Gothic houses; the **House at the Sign of the Stone Table** with its prominent Rococo features; **Liechtenstein Palace**, dating from the late 16th century; and the 17th century, late Renaissance **Town Hall of Malá Strana** (the stone plaque on its façade commemorates the promulgation of the *Confessio Bohema* in 1575).

Vrtba Palace (*Vrtbovský palác*) - This building was restructured according to the canons of late Renaissance architecture in the first half of the 17th century. The **Garden** of the same name represents a fine example of Baroque garden and is one of the most important in central Europe. It was designed by F.M. Kaňka, and built in the first half of the 18th century. Observe the statues of *Ceres* and *Bacchus*, of the same period, by M. Braun, the double staircase with Baroque decorations and sculptures inspired by Greek mythology. A beautiful view can be enjoyed from the upper terrace.

Church of St Nicholas in Malá Strana (*Chrám svatého Mikuláše*) - This splendid example of Bohemian Baroque architecture - previously belonging to the Jesuits who made it the focal point of the Counter-Reformation in Bohemia - was built on the site of a Gothic church. Work on the building started at the beginning of the 18th century and lasted until 1756 when A. Lurago completed the Bell Tower (79m). The magnificent two-tier Baroque **façade** is decorated with the coats of arms of the Count of Kolovrat and *Statues of the Fathers of the Church* carried out by followers of J.B. Kohl.

Dome and bell tower of St Nicholas in Malá Strana.

The chancel and the high Dome (75 m) are the work of K.I. Dientzenhofer. The **interior** contains some magnificent Baroque ornaments, and the ceiling of the central nave was beautifully painted with frescoes by J.L. Kracker (18th century). These show *Episodes from the Life of St Nicholas* and are some of the largest of their kind in Europe. The dome bears the splendid contemporary fresco (*Apotheosis of St Nicholas* and *Last Judgement*) by F.X. Palko who is also responsible for the frescoes in the chancel, painted in collaboration with J. Hager. I. Platzer the Elder is the author of the sculptures situated in the central nave, the chancel and at the high altar (*St Nicholas*). Also note the 18th century pulpit by Richard and Peter Prachner, the grandiose, modern organ by T. Schwarz, as well as the altar-pieces and the paintings in the side chapels (works by J.L. Kracker, I. Raab, F.X. Palko, and F. Solimena). Adjoining the church is the **Cloister** of a 13th-14th century Minorite convent.

Nostitz Palace (*Nostický palác*) - Now the seat of the Dutch Embassy, this building looks onto *Maltézské náměstí*. It was built in Baroque style in the second half of the 17th century, designed by F. Caratti who was commissioned by J.H. von Nostitz. The palace was completed in the 18th century with the addition of dormer windows with a balustrade, *Statues of the Emperors* from the Brokoff workshop (those on show today are copies), and the Rococo portal mounted between coupled columns, the work of A. Haffenecker. Inside the palace, observe the rooms used to house the **Dobrovsky Library** (painted with frescoes showing mythological themes), and the fine courtyard.

Malá Strana, steps leading up to the Castle (from Nerudova).

Grand Priory of the Knights of Malta (*Palác maltézského velkopřevora*) - Originally a Renaissance building, this construction was transformed in the first half of the 18th century by Bartolomeo Scotti who added ornamental cornices, oriel windows and the doorway. The palace now holds an interesting collection of musical instruments, part of the **Music Department of the National Museum**. Note the rich furnishings of the Baroque interiors, the inlaid flooring, the Baroque ceramic heaters and the wooden panelling.

Buquoy Palace (*Buquoyský palác*) - Currently the French Embassy, this building was designed by G. Santini and F.M. Kaňka in the first half of the 18th century on behalf of Marie Josefa von Thun. It was subsequently extended and decorated with sculptures by M.B. Braun. When the Buquoys took over as the new owners of the palace, it was furnished in Baroque style. In the latter half of the 19th century, J. Schulz added the staircase and the rear wing, in keeping with the characteristics of neo-Renaissance style. Some splendid 16th and 18th century wall-hangings can be seen in one of the rooms. The whole palace was renovated at the beginning of the 20th century. The adjoining park slopes right down to Kampa Island.

THE KARLŮV MOST (CHARLES BRIDGE) AREA

KARLŮV MOST - KAMPA - KŘIŽOVNICKÉ NÁMĚSTÍ - SMETANOVO NÁBŘEŽÍ

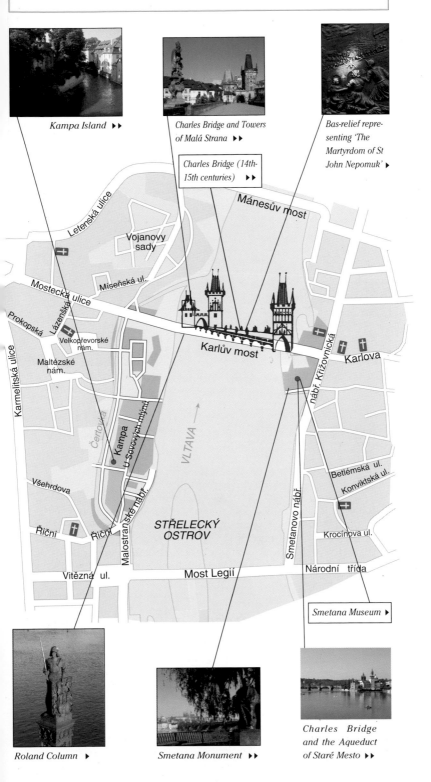

Kampa Island ▶▶

Charles Bridge and Towers of Malá Strana ▶▶

Charles Bridge (14th-15th centuries) ▶▶

Bas-relief representing 'The Martyrdom of St John Nepomuk' ▶

Roland Column ▶

Smetana Monument ▶▶

Smetana Museum ▶

Charles Bridge and the Aqueduct of Staré Mesto ▶▶

Charles Bridge viewed from the Tower of Staré Mĕsto.

One of the Charles Bridge's many sculptures.

Charles Bridge, view towards the Towers of Malá Strana.

Karlův most - The "Charles Bridge" is one of Prague's symbols *par excellence*. It joins the historic quarters of Staré Město and Malá Strana. Work was begun on its construction at the time of Charles IV (latter half of the 14th century) by P. Parler and J. Ottl, and it was completed in the early 15th century, under the reign of Wenceslas IV. The strain of the centuries and the destructive floods of the Vtlava have certainly put the Charles Bridge to the test, and in fact two of its arches had to be rebuilt in 1890. The pedestrian bridge, which affords fantastic views of the city, is 516m long, 10m wide and is supported by 16 pillars. It is watched over by mighty towers at both ends, and the whole bridge was once part of the

View of Charles Bridge towards the Tower of Staré Město.

defensive works of Prague. Its monumental Gothic feel is softened and enlivened by what we might call a genuine open-air sculpture gallery: there are as many as 30 statues and groups of sculptures on show, contributing to the magical atmosphere of Prague and the splendid views. In 1657, following the restoration of a bronze *Crucifix* which had stood here since the 14th century, statues and sculptural groups began to be placed along the parapet of the bridge: 26 of them between 1706 and 1714. Among the artists who have displayed their talents here are J. Brokoff and sons, M.B. Braun, and Josef and Emanuel Max. The group of *St Cyril and St Methodius* was sculpted in 1928 by K. Dvořák. Most of the statues have been replaced with copies since the originals are made of sandstone which is easily damaged by pollution. These are therefore kept in the Lapidarium of the National Museum. The *Statue of St Luitgard* is the most valuable one, while the figure of *St Philip Benizzi* is the only work in marble. The only bronze statue is that of *St John Nepomuk*, situated at the centre of the bridge. It is a 17th century work based on models by M. Rauchmüller and J. Brokoff. A relief carving between the sixth and seventh

Kampa Island, view over the Čertovka.

Křižovnické náměstí, Tower of Staré Město.

pillar shows where the saint was hurled into the river. A Hebrew epigraph, close to the *Crucifixion Group*, commemorates the sacrilegious act of a Jewish blasphemer (1696). A scroll situated below the 19th century Statue of *St Francis Seraphicus* bears the verses of Psalm 90/11: "God will put his angels in charge of you to protect you wherever you go". Near to the bridge (on Kampa Island) is the *Roland Column,* a 19th century copy of the 16th century original. The bridge is one of the focal points of tourist Prague: it is forever crowded with a babel of visitors, while artists, vendors and craftsmen offer their work for sale in an atmosphere reminiscent of the Parisian *Rive Gauche*. The **Towers of Malá Strana** mark the end of the bridge where it meets the quarter of the same name. The lower of the two towers, from the late 12th century, formed part of the old Judith Bridge. Some architectural and ornamental reconstruction work was carried out on it towards the end of the 16th century. The higher tower, built in the second half of the 15th century, was ordered by Jiří of Poděbrady and took the place of an old Romanesque tower. The **Tower of Staré Město** stands watch over the entrance to the bridge on the right bank of the Vtlava, where the quarter of the same name lies. Its construction was begun in the late 14th century and completed at the time of Wenceslas IV, under the direction of P. Parler. The elegant beauty of this Gothic tower is magnified by the wealth of sculptures and statues which decorate it. These are considered to represent some of the finest examples of 14th century Gothic sculpture in Bohemia (they include coats of arms, heraldic emblems, figures of saints, sovereigns and patrons of Bohemia). The Gothic paintings were restored in the 19th century, as was the whole tower which was given the roof we see today.

Waterworks and Aqueduct Tower of Staré Mĕsto.

Kampa - This island, mostly given over to parkland, stretches between the two bridges, Most Legií and Mánesův most. The Čertovka, a branch of the Vtlava which leads off to the left of the main course of the river, separates Kampa Island from the picturesque quarter of Malá Strana. During Medieval times the waters of this branch of the Vtlava fed several water mills. To the west the Karlův most rests on the island, and looking south from the bridge along the Čertovka the wheel of an old mill can be seen; to the north the stream runs through the charming area known as the 'Venice of Prague', with its characteristic canals and picturesque houses.

Křižovnické námĕstí (*Knights of the Cross Square*) - This square begins at the eastern end of Charles Bridge. It was created in the 16th century and was part of the route followed by the coronation processions of the Bohemian sovereigns. It is distinguished by the *Statue of Charles IV*, cast in iron in the first half of the 19th century. The **Church of the Holy Saviour**, once part of the *Clementinum* (situated next to the church), is a Jesuit temple, built between the 16th and 17th centuries in Renaissance style. The porch in front of the main portal was added in the 17th century by C. Lurago and F. Carati; the sculptures and vases which decorate it are the work of J.J. Bendl. The addition of the towers in the 18th century marked the completion of the church's construction. The **interior** boasts a 17th century ceiling fresco (*The four quarters of the World*, by K. Kovář). The *Charles IV Monument* (1848) is situated between the Tower of Staré Mesto and the **Church of St Francis Seraphicus at the Knights of the Cross.** The plans for this Baroque church were drawn up by J.B. Mathey, and building was completed in the second half of the 17th century. The temple, which was built on the site of an earlier Gothic church, is distinguished by its elegant dome and its **façade**, inspired by French Pre-Classicism. The statues near the entrance (*Madonna* and *St John Nepomuk*) are by M.W. Jäckel. Other sculptures on the façade represent *Angels* and *Patron Saints of Bohemia*. The **interior** is richly decorated, and the dome bears a fresco of the *Last Judgement* by V.V. Reiner (18th century). The nearby *Vintners' Column* bears a *Statue of St Wenceslas* (17th century).

Smetanovo nábřeží - The embankment is named after the 19th century composer B. Smetana; it leads from the National Theatre to a peninsular facing Charles Bridge. Of particular interest, besides the *Monument to Francis I* and the 15th century **Aqueduct Tower of Staré Město**, is the old 19th century Waterworks for its architectural design and the *sgraffiti* used to decorate it. The **Smetana Museum** Is housed here, with exhibits regarding the musician. On the quay facing the museum is the *Smetana Monument*, erected in 1984 by J. Malejovský.

Smetanovo nábřeží, Smetana Monument.

THE STARÉ MESTO (OLD TOWN) AREA

Clementinum - Church of St Clement - Mariánské náměstí - **Staroměstské náměstí** - **Old Town Hall** - **Astronomical Clock** - Goltz-Kinský Palace - House At the Stone Bell - House At the Golden Unicorn - Storch House - **Church of Our Lady of Týn** - **Church of St Nicholas in Staré Město** - Kafka's Birthplace

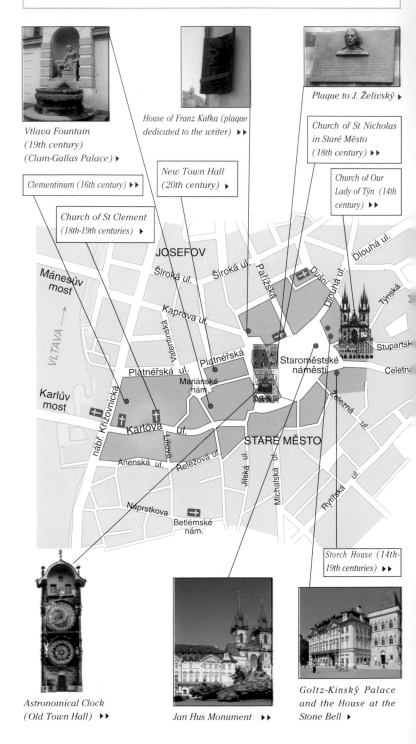

Vtlava Fountain (19th century) (Clam-Gallas Palace) ▶

House of Franz Kafka (plaque dedicated to the writer) ▶▶

Plaque to J. Želivský ▶

Church of St Nicholas in Staré Město (18th century) ▶▶

Clementinum (16th century) ▶▶

New Town Hall (20th century) ▶

Church of Our Lady of Týn (14th century) ▶▶

Church of St Clement (18th-19th centuries) ▶

Storch House (14th-19th centuries) ▶▶

Astronomical Clock (Old Town Hall) ▶▶

Jan Hus Monument ▶▶

Goltz-Kinský Palace and the House at the Stone Bell ▶

The square and rooftops of Staré Město from the Old Town Hall Tower.

Clementinum (*Klementinum*) - Formerly the Jesuit College, this building is considered to be the most impressive architectural complex in the capital, after the Castle. An entire quarter, including elegant homes, and churches and gardens, was demolished in the second half of the 16th century in order to make way for the complex. The reason for this was to support the Jesuit apostolate in their efforts to expand and consolidate Catholicism in Prague. This grandiose scheme of urban reconstruction was planned by F. Caratti and F.M. Kaňka. The 17th century main **façade** is decorated with stucco ornaments and busts of *Roman Emperors*. The **interior** houses the **National Library** (numbering more than five million volumes, 6000 manuscripts, including the valuable *Vyšehrad Codex*, and 4000 incunabula. The *Hall of the Jesuit Library* is decorated with ceiling

Clementinum, National Library, an antique codex.

frescoes (*Biblical Themes, Muses*); *The Mozart Hall* and the former *Chapel of Mirrors* are noted for their pictorial decoration; the *Hall of Mathematics* contains a collection of globes and antique table clocks. Also of interest, in the south-western courtyard (not always open), is the *Statue of the Prague Student*, in memory of those who defended the Charles Bridge at the end of the Thirty Years' War.

Church of St Clement (*Kostel svatého Klimenta*) - This church was erected between the 18th and 19th centuries within the *Clementinum* complex. An iron gate connects it to the nearby **Italian Chapel** which belongs to Prague's Italian community. The Baroque Church of St Clement is the place of worship for the Greek-Uniat community. The **interior** contains a cycle of sculptures by M.B. Braun (*Fathers of the Church, Evangelists*), considered some of the most remarkable works of Bohemian Baroque. The altar piece shows *St Linhart* (P. Brandl).

Mariánské náměstí - This square was once the site of the Church of St Mary in the Marsh. Over the centuries it has been subjected to considerable reconstruction work. The **New Town Hall**, on the eastern side of the square, is distinguished by its late Art Nouveau features. It was built in the first half of the 20th century. The statues at the entrance and the allegorical relief are the work of S. Sucharda, while the groups of *Modesty, Strength* and *Perseverance* on the balcony are by J. Mařatka. Two statues of interest, situated high up at the sides of the façade, represent *The Iron Knight* and *Rabbi Löw*.

Clam-Gallas Palace, overlooking the southern part of the square, is a splendid example of Baroque art, designed by the Viennese J.B. Fisher von

Staroměstské náměstí, Hus Monument and the Church of Our Lady of Týn.

A typical shop on Karlova.

Erlach. The building now houses the Prague city archives. M. Braun and C. Carlone were among those who contributed to the decoration of the palace with sculptures and paintings. Note the 19th century *Vtlava Fountain* by V. Prachner, situated close to the wall of the courtyard.

The **Civic Library** occupies the northern side of *Mariánské náměstí*. It was inaugurated in 1928 and stocked with over 750,000 volumes. Observe the allegorical statues by L. Kofránek, situated on the balcony.

Staroměstské náměstí - This huge square is the living heart of old Prague. Its historical importance, on the right bank of the Vtlava, can be compared to that of the Castle on the opposite side of the river. *Staroměstské náměstí* is not merely an impressive blend of architectural styles and monuments; it represents the very essence of the city itself. It has been the setting for the many events, both happy and tragic, which have marked Prague's long history: in 1422 the preacher J. Želivský was executed here (a plaque commemorates the event); in 1621 the leaders of the Protestant revolt were executed (see commemorative plaque); in 1915 the bronze *Jan Hus Monument* was inaugurated, on the occasion of the 5th centenary of his death (the work is by L. Šaloun, and an epigraph reads *The truth will win*); in 1945 the people of Prague joyfully welcomed the Soviet army at the end of the Second World War; in 1968 the crowd bombarded Soviet tanks with Molotov cocktails for shattering the dream of the "Prague Spring", and the Hus Monument was veiled as a sign of mourning; in 1988 the people of Prague demanded freedom, civil rights and the removal of the "brothers" of the Warsaw Pact; and in 1990 the square was one of the settings for the "Velvet Revolution" which marked a return to democracy. The square at night, with its carefully studied illumination, is especially charming: the lights create surreal, fantastic, almost fairy-tale dimensions on the façades of the noble buildings and up towards the incredible spires of the Church of Our Lady of Týn. All around, in the square and along *Karlova*, jugglers and musicians brighten the city's evenings, again offering a typically "Parisian" image.

Old Town Hall, Křiž House.

Old Town Hall (*Staroměstská radnice*) - The history of this building begins in the 11th century and continues uninterruptedly, through various periods of extension, damage, destruction and reconstruction, right up until the last restoration work carried out between 1978 and 1981. The original central part of the building was constructed in 1338; a tower was then added in 1364. Křiž House was built before this, in 1360, and stands out today because of its lively paintwork and the epigraph *Praga caput regni*. Serious damage was inflicted on the complex at the end of the Second World War. The *Council Chamber* has maintained its Gothic character which originates from the second half of the 15th century. The huge *Meeting Hall* contains paintings by V. Brožík (*Jiří Poděbrady elected King of Bohemia, J. Hus before the Council of Constance*). There is a charming view from the top of the 69m high **Old Town Hall Tower**, which can be reached by lift.

Astronomical Clock (*Orloj*) - The clock was built by Master Mikuláš of Kadan and was mounted in the lower part of the Old Town Hall Tower at the beginning of the 15th century. At the end of the century Master Hanuš took charge of its rebuilding, and in the second half of the 16th century it was perfected and enlarged by J. Táborský. Every hour the charming *Procession of Apostles* appears with its eloquent allegories, attracting the surprised attention of tourists and visitors who crowd round in the attractive little square below.

Old Town Hall, Astronomical Clock.

Goltz Kinský Palace (*Palác Goltz-Kinskych*) - This impressive late Baroque palace, which animates the eastern side of the square with

Astronomical Clock, allegorical figures (detail).

its Rococo and neo-classical designs, is the result of the joining together of a Romanesque building and an early Gothic house. Count J.E. Goltz entrusted the project to K.I. Dientzenhofer, while the actual building work was carried out by A. Lurago in the latter half of the 18th century. It was subsequently acquired by Prince R. Kinský. Note the **façade** and its interesting features: the pilaster strips, the triangular tympanums, the long balcony resting on the columns situated on either side of the portals, the windows decorated with stuccowork and Rococo patterns, and the statues

Astronomical Clock, signs of the zodiac and allegorical figures.

Storch House, detail of the façade.

situated on the attic. The palace houses the **National Gallery Collection of Graphic Art**.

House at the Stone Bell (*'U kamenného zvonu'*) - The building's elegant Gothic **façade** was only restored to the public eye in the 1960s when some reconstruction work brought it to light underneath a dubious late 19th century addition. The house's origins date back to the 13th century, and its name is already mentioned in records of the 15th century. Its appearance was then gradually altered until no trace remained of the beautiful building which, however, visitors can now admire again.

House at the Golden Unicorn (*'U zlatého jednorožce'*) - This building, at n° 20, was extended as early as the 14th century, and towards the end of the following century it was rebuilt in late-Gothic style. The **façade** bears the hallmark of late Baroque and dates from the 18th century. A plaque here commemorates the famous composer, B. Smetana, who opened his first music school in this house.

Storch House - This lovely building, situated at the lower end of the square at n° 16, close to *Celetná ulice*, is distinguished by its beautiful decorations and the architectural details which ennoble the fine **façade**. The painting which adorns the façade, and which recalls the type of fresco-decorated houses common among the aristocratic residences of central Europe, depicts *St Wenceslas on horseback*. Originally a 14th-15th century Gothic residence, Storch House was restored in neo-Renaissance style towards the end of the 19th century and remains as such today. The building next door, known as the **House at the Stone Ram** (n° 17), is also called *At the Unicorn* because of the subject of the bas-relief which decorates the façade.

Church of Our Lady of Týn (*Kostel Panny Marie pred Týnem*) - This mighty construction, one of the capital's most famous symbols, rises high above the rooftops of old Prague. The present day building was erected on the site of an earlier Romanesque church in the second half of the 14th century, and the choir was completed towards the end of that century. The **façade**, in all its austere, Gothic magnificence, was completed in the second half of the 15th century at the request of Jíří of Poděbrady. The tympanum contains a

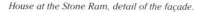
House at the Stone Ram, detail of the façade.

Statue of the Madonna, and the façade is dominated by twin bell towers, although these were built at different times (the northern one in the 15th century and the southern one in the 16th century). They are both 80 m high and crowned with soaring pinnacles and angular turrets which contribute to the fairy-tale setting. The high, majestic **interior** is distinguished by the mighty pillars which separate the three naves and support the imposing ogival arches. The ceiling above the naves is formed of cross-vaults. Fine wooden altars with gold-leaf work stand against the pillars.

Staré Město square and the Church of Our Lady of Týn, viewed from the Old Town Hall Tower.

The Church also contains the *Tomb of Tycho Brahe*, Court Astronomer to Rudolph II; a Gothic *Madonna and Child* (15th century); and the late Gothic baldachin by M. Rejsek (late 15th century). The paintings on the high altar (*Holy Trinity* and *Assumption of the Virgin*) are by Karel Škréta (17th century).

Madonna on gold background (Church of Our Lady of Týn, detail of tympanum).

45

Church of St Nicholas in Staré Město (*Kostel svatého Mikuláše*) - This masterpiece of Baroque architecture was built in the first half of the 18th century by K.I. Dientzenhofer. The monumental south-facing **façade** is a triumph of exquisite Baroque architectural and ornamental patterns. The twin bell towers, the dome and the central part of the façade are of a singular elegance. The **interior** consists of a central nave with side chapels. The ceiling paintings, showing the *Lives of St Nicholas and St Benedict,* and the frescoes in the side chapels and presbytery are the work of P. Asam the Elder. The *Statue of St Nicholas* on the side façade was added at the beginning of the 20th century and is by B. Šimonovský.

Franz Kafka's Birthplace (*U věže*) - Not far from the church, at n° 5 *U radnice*, stands the house where Franz Kafka was born. A *Bust* of the famous Prague writer (1883-1924) can be seen here.

The Baroque façade of the Church of St Nicholas in Staré Město.

Church of St Nicholas in Staré Město, detail of the dome (interior).

View of Franz Kafka's birthplace.

THE JOSEFOV AREA

THE GHETTO - OLD JEWISH CEMETERY - **STATE JEWISH MUSEUM** - SYNAGOGUES - MUSEUM OF APPLIED ART - THE HOUSE OF ARTISTS - ST AGNES'S CONVENT

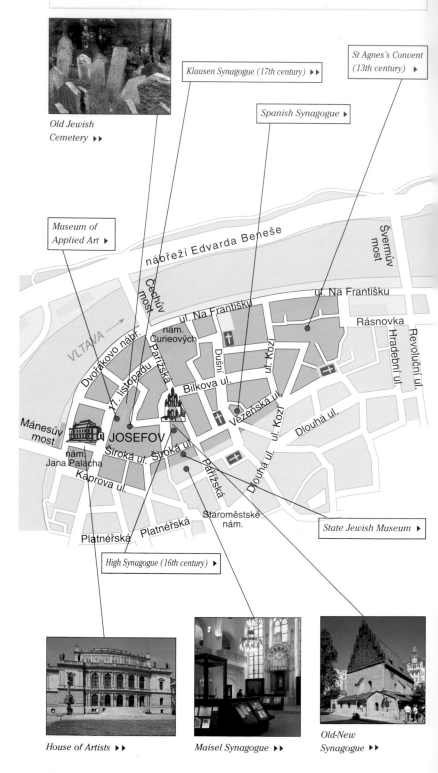

Old Jewish Cemetery ▶▶

Klausen Synagogue (17th century) ▶▶

St Agnes's Convent (13th century) ▶

Spanish Synagogue ▶

Museum of Applied Art ▶

State Jewish Museum ▶

High Synagogue (16th century) ▶

House of Artists ▶▶

Maisel Synagogue ▶▶

Old-New Synagogue ▶▶

The Ghetto (*židovské ghetto***)** - Prague's old Jewish Ghetto occupies a part of the Staré Město quarter and is important both in terms of its size, and the cultural and tourist interest it provokes. The *Josefov* quarter takes its name from the Emperor Joseph II. The first Jewish settlements in Prague appeared around the 10th century, and by the 17th century more than 7000 Jews had made the city their home. Persecutions, fires and plundering were regular occurrences throughout the centuries, making life difficult for the Jewish community. Towards the middle of the 18th century Maria Theresa of Habsburg decreed that the Jews should be driven out. Later that century, however, the Emperor Joseph II had the walls of the Ghetto demolished, restoring both the Jewish quarter itself, and its administrative status. The area was named Josefov in his honour. Jews were not granted Civil rights until 1848. The period of Nazi occupation in Prague (1939-1945) was the darkest time for the Jewish community whose members became the object of persecutions and deportations. It is estimated that 90% of Bohemian and Moravian Jews were killed during the Second World War. The group of buildings, used for religious and non-religious purposes, which, together with the cemetery, make up the Ghetto, has now been transformed into a kind of large open-air museum. One of the most beautiful architectural features of the Ghetto is the **Jewish Town Hall** (*Židovská radnice*), a Renaissance building which dates from the second half of the 16th century. It was remodelled in Baroque style in the lat-

Partial view of the Jewish Town Hall.

49

Hebrew inscription in Josefov.

ter half of the 18th century, and extended at the beginning of the 20th century. Note the unusual clock situated in the tympanum, under the small clock tower: it has Hebrew figures and the hands move in an anticlockwise direction.

Old Jewish Cemetery (*Starý židovský hřbitov*) - The fact that makes this site so interesting, and one of the most visited places on the tourist trail, is the incredible number of gravestones it holds, about 20,000 of them. Because of the lack of available space, they are all packed tightly together, stone upon stone in a picturesque fashion, giving the place a fascinating atmosphere. It is said that in some parts of the cemetery there are at least

Old Jewish Cemetery, Tomb of Rabbi Löw.

nine layers of burials. The Hebrew epigraphs and the reliefs which decorate the tombstones give an interesting insight into the Jewish community of the time, since, apart from the sex and marital status of the deceased, they also record connections with a particular art, trade or social class of any importance, such as that of a priest. The cemetery, which was founded in the first half of the 15th century, continued to be used as such at least until the second half of the 18th century.

State Jewish Museum (*Státní Židovské muzeum*) - The collections which make up the framework of the museum, and which allow us to understand the development of the city's Jewish community and its culture, originate from various synagogues in Bohemia, Moravia, and Europe in general. Despite the fact that the Nazis wanted to make it into the "Exotic museum of an extinct race", the number of exhibits increased considerably precisely during the period of the occupation of Prague.

Synagogues - There are many synagogues in the Jewish quarter. The **High Synagogue** (*Vysaká synagóga*) was built in the second half of the 16th century, to a design by P. Roder. In the 19th century restoration work was carried out to separate it from the Town Hall. The central, square hall, originally Renaissance in style, was transformed in the 17th-19th centuries and remodelled in neo-Renaissance style. Note the magnificent stellar vaulting. The rooms of the synagogue are used for exhibitions by the State Jewish Museum (they contain vestments, manuscripts and precious ornaments).
The **Old-New Synagogue** (*Staronová synagóga*), originally Gothic in design, was extended in Cistercian Gothic style in the 13th century. Further modifications and additions were completed between the 15th and 18th centuries. Renovation and restoration work was also carried out in the 19th-20th centuries. The synagogue is still used for religious functions. A *Statue of Moses* by F. Bílek can be seen in the adjoining park.

The unique architecture of the Old-New Synagogue.

Interior of the Klausen Synagogue.

The 17th century **Klausen Synagogue** (*Klausova synagóga*) is built on the site once occupied by the Jewish School of Löw ben Bezalel, a 16th century Rabbi and philosopher. The Baroque building houses a collection of prints and manuscripts.

The earliest religious building on the site of today's **Pinkas Synagogue** (*Pinkasova synagóga),* probably a ritual bath, is said to date from the 11th-12th centuries. In the first half of the 16th century a late Gothic synagogue was constructed in the building which had been the home of Rabbi Pinkas (hence the modern name). This was rebuilt and enlarged in the first half of the 17th century, in late Renaissance style. In the 1950s the synagogue

Interior of the Maisel Synagogue.

became the seat of the *Memorial of the 77, 297*, a monument erected in memory of the victims of the Holocaust.

The building which today houses the **Spanish Synagogue** (*Španelská synagóga*) bears some striking Moorish features, added in the second half of the 19th century. The temple interior is strongly reminiscent of the Alhambra in Granada. The synagogue owes its name to a community of Iberian Jews who came to Prague to escape persecution. It has been destroyed by fire and rebuilt several times, and occupies the site of the Old School, the oldest synagogue in the city (12th century).

The **Maisel Synagogue** (*Maiselova synagóga*) takes its name from the mayor of the Jewish quarter at the time of Rudolph II. It was built in Renaissance style at the end of the 16th century, and reconstructed in Baroque style about a century later, after a fire. The building as it appears today was restored in neo-Gothic style between the 19th and 20th centuries. The interior houses the splendid exhibition of *Silver from Bohemian Synagogues*, including interesting examples of Baroque and Rococo art by Augsburg, Nuremberg and Viennese craftsmen, as well as decorations and treasures from various eras, collected from synagogues and private homes.

Museum of Applied Art (*Umělecko-prûmyslové muzeum*) - This neo-Renaissance construction, designed by J. Schulz and built between the end of the 19th and the beginning of the 20th century, is situated close to the Old Jewish Cemetery. Some of the most notable exhibits in the museum include furnishings and furniture, goldsmith's work, porcelain, crystal and pottery, textiles, bronzes, measuring instruments and a minter. The Library contains some 15th century parchments.

House of Artists (*Dům umělcu*) - This grandiose construction, with its elegant architectural forms, stands majestically on the banks of the Vtlava and overlooks the square named after *Jan Palach*, the martyr of the "Prague Spring" in 1968. It is also known as the *Rudolfinum*, as it was named in honour of Rudolph of Habsburg. It was built in the second half of the 19th century by J. Žítek and J. Schulz. Once the seat of the Czechoslovak Parliament (1919-1939), it is considered to be one of the most outstanding examples of neo-Renaissance architecture in Prague. An allegory dedicated to Wagner adorns the main entrance, while the

Statue of Josef Mânes.

53

The neo-Renaissance façade of the House of Artists.

balustrade is decorated with statues of illustrious artists and musicians. Of particular interest inside the building is the sumptuously decorated *Dvořák Hall*. Close to the river is the *Statue of Josef Mánes*, by B. Kafka (1951). The nearby *Mánesův most* is also named after this Czech artist.

St Agnes's Convent (*Anežský klášter*) - This building, which now houses collections of the National Gallery and the Museum of Applied Art, ranks among the most important historical constructions in the capital. Its building was requested in the first half of the 13th century by Princess Agnes, sister of King Wenceslas I, whose intention it was to provide a seat for the Poor Clares. She subsequently took her vows in the Order of St Clare and became the first Abbess of the new convent. A crescendo of building activity followed, giving rise to the **Minorite Monastery** (1240); the **Church of St Barbara** (14th century, and renewed in Baroque style in the 17th century. The tombs of *King Wenceslas I, St Agnes*, and several Přemyslid sovereigns have been found here); the **Church of St Francis** (mid 13th century) with its Franciscan Monastery; and the **Church of the Holy Saviour** (latter half of the 13th century), an outstanding example of Early Bohemian Gothic. It is said to have been the burial place of the Přemyslids.
Some of the most interesting collections housed in the rebuilt and restored convent complex are the paintings of Bohemian history (19th century) and the works of artistic craftsmanship.

THE CELETNÁ ULICE AND VÁCLAVSKÉ NÁMĚSTÍ AREAS

CELETNÁ ULICE - CAROLINUM - ESTATES THEATRE - CHURCH OF ST JAMES - **POWDER TOWER** - MUNICIPAL HOUSE - **NA PŘÍKOPĚ** - **VÁCLAVSKÉ NÁMĚSTÍ** - NATIONAL MUSEUM - CHURCH OF OUR LADY OF THE SNOWS

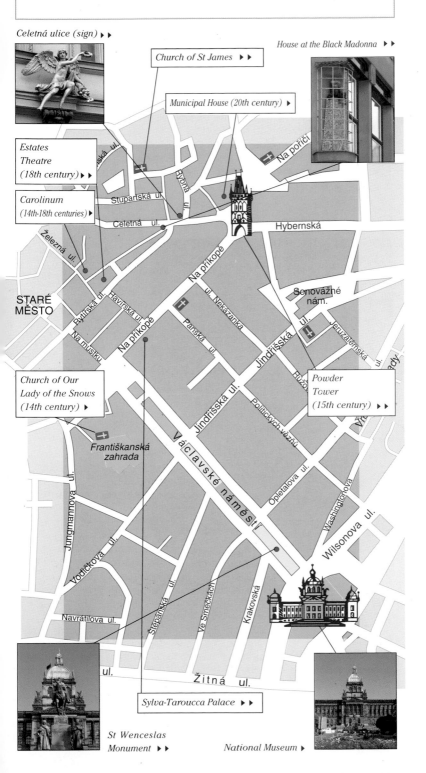

Celetná ulice (sign) ▸ ▸

House at the Black Madonna ▸ ▸

Church of St James ▸ ▸

Municipal House (20th century) ▸

Estates
Theatre
(18th century) ▸ ▸

Carolinum
(14th-18th centuries) ▸

STARÉ
MĚSTO

Church of Our
Lady of the Snows
(14th century) ▸

Powder
Tower
(15th century) ▸ ▸

Františkanská
zahrada

Sylva-Taroucca Palace ▸ ▸

St Wenceslas
Monument ▸ ▸

National Museum ▸

55

Celetná ulice - In the second half of the 1980s this important thoroughfare of Staré Město regained some of its past grandeur. It became and remained an important route in ancient times, and was also on the route followed by the coronation processions of Bohemian sovereigns. Today the *Celetná ulice* is noted for the majestic, Baroque constructions which line the street, the result of remodellings of earlier buildings from the Romanesque and Gothic periods. The balustrade at **Sixt House**, situated at n° 2, bears some remarkable sculptures attributed to A. Braun. At n° 12 stands the former **Hrzán Palace** with its attractive façade decorated with sculptures from the F.M. Brokoff workshop; G.B. Aliprandi was probably responsible for the reconstruction of the façade. Note the coat of arms which adorns the door of the building at n° 16. A characteristic *Vinárna* has been opened in **Menhart House** at n° 17. Some of the buildings are now used by the University of Prague (n°s 20-22). The Baroque façade of the house at n° 23 is adorned with an 18th century *Statue of the Virgin* by M.B. Braun. Note also the buildings at n° 31 (the Baroque **Pachtovský Palace**) and n° 34, the **House at the Black Madonna,** whose façade bears the sign of the *Virgin Behind Bars*. The **House at the Mint** (n° 36) is a reminder of the Mint which has stood here since the 16th century.

The Black Madonna stands out from behind bars on the corner of the building at n°34 Celetná ulice.

Carolinum - This building, which was reconstructed in Baroque style in the first half of the 18th century, still preserves some elements of the original Gothic construction, particularly noticeable in the fine oriel window which decorates the **façade**, and in the entrance. The Carolinum takes its name from King Charles IV who founded central Europe's first University here around the middle of the 14th century. The 17th century *Aula Magna* is of considerable architectural interest: it is arranged on two floors and was extended around the middle of the 20th century.

Celetná ulice, portal with Madonna.

Estates Theatre (***Stavoské divadlo***) - This was the first theatre to be built in the Bohemian capital. It was founded in fact by Count A. von Nostitz-Rieneck who entrusted its design to A. Haffenecker in the latter half of the 18th century. The theatre has changed both name and owner several times: it has now re-adopted the name which was popular from the end of the 18th century onwards, and is a part of the National Theatre. On 29th October 1787 the debut performance of W.A. Mozart's *Don Giovanni* was given here. Between 1813 and 1816 the theatre's orchestra was conducted by Carl Maria von Weber.

Partial view of the Estates Theatre.

Church of St James, Baroque stuccowork on the façade.

Church of St James (*Kostel svatého Jakuba*) - The Baroque appearance of this church is the result of a series of work carried out between the 17th and 18th centuries on an earlier Gothic building. This in its turn had replaced the original 13th century temple, itself destroyed by fire. The **façade** is embellished with fine stuccowork figures by O. Mosto; these represent *St James, St Francis*, and *St Anthony of Padua*. The temple's remarkable **interior**, divided by pillars, is extraordinarily long (in fact, it is second only to the Cathedral in this respect). It also contains some rich pictorial decoration. The ceiling paintings are by F.Q. Voget (*Scenes from the Life of the Virgin, Glorification of the Holy Trinity*), while the high altar bears the painting of the *Martyrdom of St James* by V.V. Reiner. The Baroque *Tomb of Count Vratislav of Mitrovice* was designed by J.B. Fischer von Erlach and executed by F.M. Brokoff in the 18th century. Adjoining the building is the **Cloister** of an old Minorite monastery.

Powder Tower (*Prašná brána*) - From the top of its 65m, this majestic tower dominates the important Staré Mesto crossroads where *Celetná ulice, Na příkopě,* and *Náměstí Republiky* meet. The late Gothic structure was built in the second half of the 15th century on the site of an earlier fortified gateway dating from the 13th century. It was built by M. Rejsek for Vladislav Jagiello, and was modelled on the Staré Město Bridge Tower, forming one of the strongholds of the defence system. The name of the tower derives from a gunpowder store located here in the 18th century. Note the coats of arms which decorate it, together with the statues of *Bohemian Saints and Sovereigns*. Fine views can be had from the top, which is reached by a spiral staircase.

Powder Tower, one of the symbols of Staré Město.

Na příkopě, the fine Sylva-Taroucca Palace.

Municipal House (*Representační dům hlavního města Prahy*) - This building is one of the most prominent examples of Art Nouveau in Prague. It was built on the site of momentous historical events (in the second half of the first decade of the 20th century), and its **façade** (K. Novák) bears some striking ornamentation, enriched with allegories by L. Šaloun. The *Smetana Hall* (used for concerts) is one of the most interesting parts of the interior; the podium is decorated with frescoes once again by L. Šaloun (*Bohemian Dances, Vyšehrad*). Among the building's other halls, painted with frescoes and richly decorated, note in particular the *Primátor Hall, Rieger Hall, Palacký Hall, Grégor Hall* and *Sladkovský Hall*.

Na příkopě - Situated at the heart of the *Golden Cross*, this is Prague's lively commercial centre, full of shops, banks, restaurants and office blocks. Its Czech name means "by the moat" (in fact, *Na příkopě* lies along the path of a moat which divided Staré Město - the "Old Town" - from Nové Mesto - the "New Town"); a stream once flowed in its bed. At n° 4 is the 19th century building which houses **Dům elegance**, the oldest department store in the Capital, built by T. Hansen at the end of the 19th century. Opposite this is the modern building of **ČKD Praha**, built at the beginning of the 1980s. At n° 10 is the **Sylva-Taroucca Palace**, a splendid example of Bohemian Baroque architecture. It was designed by K.I. Dientzenhofer, and built by A. Lurago. The building's decoration was carried out by I. Platzer the Elder and C. Bassi, among others. The building at n° 15 is a children's store, designed in the Constructivist style, remodelled by L. Kysela at the end of the 1930s, and renovated in 1950. The Piarist church of the **Holy Cross** was designed by J. Fischer in the first half of the 19th century; it is the only neo-classical church in Prague. The **Čedok** office (Czech Tourist Office) is at n° 18. The building at n° 20, in marked Bohemian Renaissance style, is decorated with bas-relief work and allegorical mosaics. It houses the Prague Information Service. Also worthy of note are the **Casa Slava**, originally Baroque in design (17th-18th centuries) and renovated in neo-classical style at the end of the 19th century, and the **State Bank Building** at n° 24, erected in the late 1930s. Previously on this site stood some famous hotels where illustrious figures of the 19th centu-

Scenic view of Wenceslas Square.

ry used to stay. The *Náměstí Republiky* is situated close by, overlooked by the modern building which houses the department store **Kotva** at n° 8. This is considered to be one of the best stocked stores in the Capital.

Václavské náměstí - The impressive *Wenceslas Square* is situated in the heart of the city. Its dimensions (750 x 60m) make it look more like a Parisian Boulevard than a square. It is a lively conglomeration of well-known hotels (like the "Evropa" at n° 25, a treasure of Art Nouveau architecture), restaurants and cafés, galleries, shops, cinemas and clubs, which together with *Na příkopě, Na Můstku* and *28 října* forms the group of main thoroughfares known as the *Golden Cross*. This is the commercial heart of the Czech metropolis, redeveloped in the 1980s to include wide green spaces, following the building of the underground system. In the square, opposite the National Museum, stands the *St Wenceslas Monument,* the work of J.V. Myslbek (1912-1913). The patron saint of Bohemia is represented on horseback, surrounded by the statues of *St Ludmilla, St Procopius* and *St Adalbert of Prague*. The square was originally founded as a horse market by Charles IV, at the same time as Nové Město; it was given its present name towards the middle of the 19th century. Wenceslas Square also represents the moral and historical conscience of the newly-formed Czech Republic. In the early months of 1969 it was the scene of dramatic events following the military occupation by troops of the Warsaw Pact (August 1968). On 16th January the Philosophy student Jan Palach burnt himself to death at the foot of the St Wenceslas Monument, and a few weeks later the student Jan Zajic committed suicide in the same square. Nineteen years later, on the 28th October 1988, the Communist police forcefully dispersed a demonstration commemorating the proclamation of the First Republic. Again in 1989 there were further incidents of brutality against demonstrators commemorating the sacrifice of Palach. These events led inevitably to the "Velvet Revolution" which, within a few months, gave back to Czechoslovakia the dignity of a free country.

National Museum (*Národní muzeum***)** - This imposing neo-Renaissance building, which stands the full width of the southern end of *Václavské náměstí*, was built in the second half of the 19th century to a design by J.

Wenceslas Square, detail of the Europa Hotel, an example of Art Nouveau in Prague.

Schulz. It houses the main seat of the National Museum, with the **Museum of History and Natural History**, and the rooms used to house the **Library** (which numbers more than 1.3 million volumes and 8000 manuscripts). The domed **Pantheon** contains various busts and statues representing important figures from Czech culture. The Mineralogy, Botany, and Zoology collections are displayed in the side wings. The Historical and Archaeological sections contain some interesting coins, medals and theatrical exhibits. The National Museum also incorporates sections of the museums dedicated to *Ethnography*, *Musical Instruments*, *Náprstek* and *Physical Culture and Sport*. These are all housed in separate buildings.

Church of Our Lady of the Snows (***Kostel Panny Marie Sněžné***) - This church was built in 1347 under the patronage of Charles IV who intended to make it the seat for coronations. Once completed, the ambitious project was supposed to surpass even the magnificence of the Cathedral of St Vitus. However, by the end of the century only the 30m high Chancel was completed. The fine Gothic portal on the northern side is decorated with an abundance of statues of saints. In the 15th century the church went into gradual decline, and in the first half of the 17th century the vaulting collapsed and had to be replaced with a Renaissance ceiling. It was used as a meeting place by the Hussite movement, and on 30th July 1419 J. Želivský and his followers stormed the Town Hall, causing the defenestration of the Catholic councillors. In fact, this first Prague defenestration marked the beginning of the Hussite Wars. The **interior** of the church contains the 17th century Baroque high altar, considered to be the largest of its kind in Prague's churches. Above the left-hand side altar is an *Annunciation* by V.V. Reiner. The pewter font dates from the second half of the 15th century.

On the next page: Wenceslas Square, an evocative nocturnal image of the Monument to the patron saint of Bohemia.

THE NATIONAL THEATRE AREA

NATIONAL THEATRE - BETHLEHEM CHAPEL - CHURCH OF ST CYRIL AND ST
METHODIUS

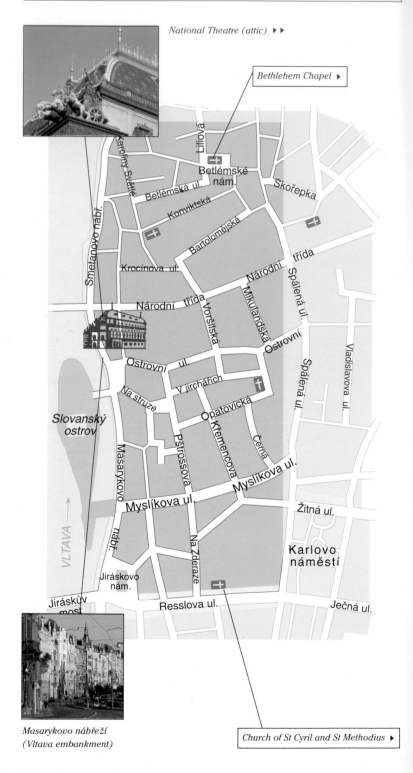

National Theatre (attic) ▶ ▶

Bethlehem Chapel ▶

Karolíny Světlé

Liliová

Betlémské
nám.

Betlémská ul.

Skořepka

Konviktská

Bartolomějská

Smetanovo nábř.

Krocínova ul.

Národní   třída

Spálená ul.

Národní   třída

Vorsílská

Mikulandská

Ostrovní

Vladislavova ul.

Ostrovní   ul.

Na struze

V jirchářích

Spálená ul.

*Slovanský
ostrov*

Opatovická

Pštrossova

Křemencova

Černá

Myslíkova ul.

Masarykovo

Myslíkova ul.

Žitná ul.

VLTAVA →

nábř.

Na Zderaze

Karlovo
náměstí

Jiráskovo
nám.

Jiráskův
most

Resslova ul.

Ječná ul.

*Masarykovo nábřeží
(Vltava embankment)*

Church of St Cyril and St Methodius ▶

National Theatre (*Národní divadlo*) - This beautiful building, with its neo-Renaissance architectural features, stands on the right bank of the Vtlava. It was erected in the second half of the 19th century to a design by J. Zítek. A short time after the staging of the very first performance the theatre was destroyed by fire and rebuilt in record time by J. Schulz, a follower of Zítek's. Careful restoration work was carried out between 1976 and 1983. The modern complex called the **New Stage** was added in 1983; this also includes the **Laterna Magica Theatre**. The northern **façade** is adorned with *Statues of Záboj and Lumír*, the work of artists from the workshop of A. Wagner. Two groups of statues adorn the attic storey, *Apollo and the Muses*, and *Goddesses of Victory*, both by B. Schnirch. *Allegories of Opera and Drama* attributed to J.V. Myslbek stand above the side entrance, and the same artist also created the busts of illustrious figures. The **interior** of the National Theatre is richly decorated with paintings. The ceiling of the auditorium bears eight *Allegories representing the Arts* by F. Ženíšek who also painted the *Golden Age, Decline and Revival of Art*, which decorates the lobby on the first balcony. The cycle of paintings (*The Homeland*) which appears in the tympanums of the arcades, and the wall paintings entitled *Pagan Myth, History, Life*, and *Folk Music* are the joint work of F. Ženíšek and M. Aleš.

Bethlehem Chapel (*Betlémská kaple*) - The building which stands here today is the result of a faithful reconstruction of the original, destroyed in the second half of the 18th century. This work was completed in the early 1950s by J. Fragner who gathered information about the original chapel from old iconographic sources, descriptions and prints of the earlier building. This had been built towards the end of the 14th century at the request of the citizens of Prague who wanted a church where they could celebrate Mass in their own language. Instead the church authorities only gave their permission for the construction of a Gothic chapel, although this was capable of accommodating a congregation of 3000. The Czech reformer Jan Hus preached from its pulpit in the first half of the 15th century, and even after his death the Bethlehem Chapel remained one of the strongholds of the Prague Hussite movement. In the first half of the 17th century the chapel belonged to the Bohemian Brotherhood, but after the Battle of the White Mountain (8th Nov 1620) it passed into the hands of the Jesuits. In 1733 the Order was dissolved and not long afterwards the building was destroyed. The **interior** contains wall paintings based on the *Velislav Bible*, the *Jena Kodex*, and the *Richenthalsch Chronicles*. Also on view are some passages from the J. Hus and J. ze Stříbro treaties.

Church of St Cyril and St Methodius (*Kostel svatého Cyrila a Metoděje*) - This building, which has been the seat of the Greek-Orthodox Church since 1935, was constructed in Baroque style to a design by K.I. Dientzenhofer. It was originally dedicated to *St Charles Borromeo*. The stuccowork which decorates the **interior** is by M.I. Palliardi. In 1942 the church was the scene of an armed confrontation between Czech parachutists and Nazi SS troops; the latter, in retaliation for the killing of the Governor of Bohemia and Moravia, had wiped out the male population of Lidice and deported its women and children. A *plaque* in the *Crypt* commemorates the sacrifice of the parachutists.

National Theatre viewed from the Vltava.

THE KARLOVO NÁMĚSTÍ (CHARLES SQUARE) AREA

Karlovo náměstí - New Town Hall - Church of St Ignatius - Faust House - Dvořák Museum (Villa America)

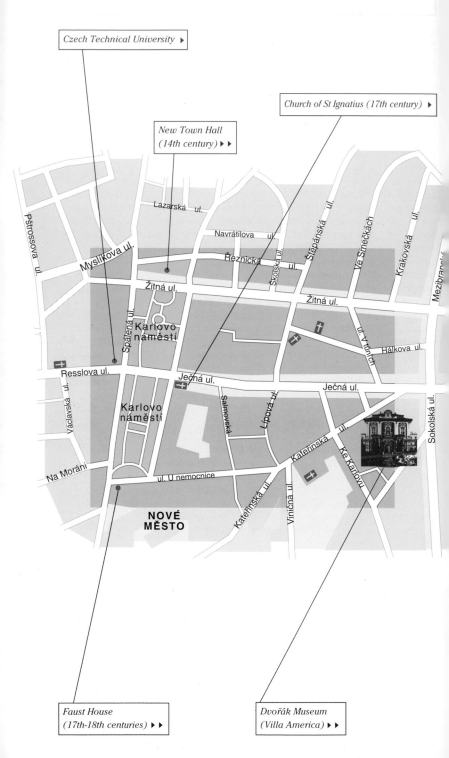

Czech Technical University ▶

Church of St Ignatius (17th century) ▶

New Town Hall
(14th century) ▶ ▶

Faust House
(17th-18th centuries) ▶ ▶

Dvořák Museum
(Villa America) ▶ ▶

Karlovo náměstí - This is the largest square in Prague (530 x 150 m), refined by gardens and trees which give it the appearance of a park, and the site of monuments which have been erected to commemorate illustrious figures from Czech culture. Up until the middle of the 19th century the cattle market was held here. Situated around the park area are a number of interesting buildings.

At n° 14 stands the **Czech Technical University**, designed in neo-Renaissance style by V.I. Ullmann. On either side of the doorway are *Allegories of Work and Science*, from the A. Popp workshop. The second floor windows are decorated with *Statues of Past Geniuses* by J.V. Myslbek.

New Town Hall (*Novoměstská radnice*) - This building was constructed around the middle of the 14th century in Gothic style. In 1784 it ceased to used as a town hall and instead became a prison, courthouse and registry office. It was also the scene of the "First Prague Defenestration" in 1419, which led to the Hussite Wars. The 15th century tower houses a chapel. Reconstruction work in the 16th century added Renaissance features to the building's southern wing, and Empire style features were added in the 19th century. At the beginning of the 20th century work was carried out to restore the tower to its original Renaissance appearance.

Church of St Ignatius (*Kostel svatého Ignáce*) - This beautiful Baroque church is noted for its fine two-tier **façade** and its magnificent late 17th century portal. Among the statues which decorate the front of the church, the *Statue of St Ignatius* by P.I. Bayer, and others by A. Soldati are worth special attention. The construction of the church dates back to the second half of the 17th century when C. Lurago drew up the plans for a place of worship for the Jesuit College. The **interior** is composed of a single nave and is richly ornate with stuccowork, decorations and paintings. The painting on the 18th century Baroque high altar depicts *The Glory of St Ignatius Loyola* (17th century, by J.G. Heintsch). The stuccowork and the statues of saints are by A. Soldati, and the painting of *Christ Imprisoned* is by K. Škréta. The painting of *St Liborius* is the work of I. Raab. Note also the *Calvary Group* by J.A. Quittainer.

Faust House (*Faustův dům*) - Also known as *Mladota Palace*, Faust House is situated on the southern side of the square at n° 40, and houses a chemist's. Originally built in late Renaissance style, it was fortified in the first half of the 17th century and later renovated in Baroque style (18th

A lofty tower dominates the New Town Hall.

View of Faust House.

century). It was here, at the time of Rudolph II, that an English alchemist called E. Kelly carried out his experiments aimed at producing gold, and in the 18th century Mladota of Solopysky set up his own alchemist's laboratory. Since then the legend of Dr Faust has been associated with this house, thus keeping the myth of "The Magical City" alive.

Dvořák Museum /Villa America (*Letohrádek America*) - Housed in the splendid setting of the Villa America, the Dvořák Museum contains music scores, documents and correspondence belonging to the Czech composer Antonín Dvořák (1841-1904). It is easy to see why the building is considered a treasure of Prague Baroque architecture. It was designed by K.I. Dientzenhofer for Count Michna who made it his magnificent summer residence. The villa, which dates from the first half of the 18th century, is also known as *Villa Michna* and is distinguished by its fine Baroque entrancegate (a copy), its 18th century frescoes by J.F. Schor, and its statues of the same era situated in the garden, from the A. Braun workshop.

The beautiful Villa America, home to the Dvořák Museum.

THE PETŘÍN HILL AREA

Church of Our Lady Victorious - Italian Hospital - **Petřín Observation Tower** - Mirror Maze - Church of St Lawrence - Observatory - **Villa Bertramka** - **Mozart Museum**

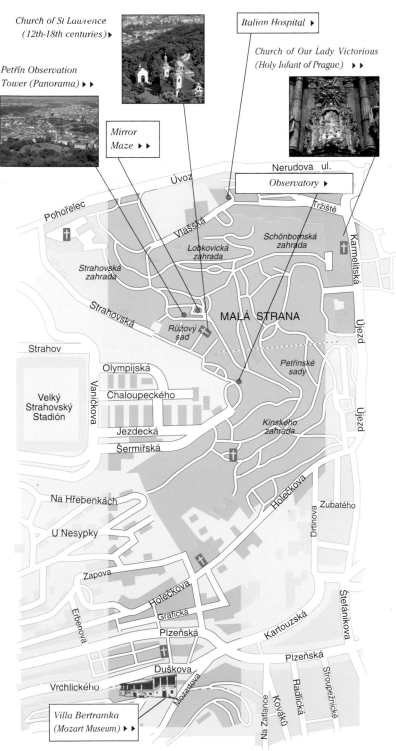

Church of St Lawrence (12th-18th centuries) ▶

Petřín Observation Tower (Panorama) ▶ ▶

Italian Hospital ▶

Church of Our Lady Victorious (Holy Infant of Prague) ▶ ▶

Mirror Maze ▶ ▶

Neruda ul.

Observatory ▶

Úvoz

Pohořelec

Vlašská

Tržiště

Schönbornská zahrada

Lobkovická zahrada

Strahovská zahrada

Karmelitská

Strahovská

Růžový sad

MALÁ STRANA

Strahov

Olympijská

Petřínské sady

Újezd

Velký Strahovský Stadión

Vaníčkova

Chaloupeckého

Jezdecká

Šermiřská

Kinského zahrada

Na Hřebenkách

Holečkova

Zubatého

U Nesypky

Drtinova

Zapova

Holečkova

Grafická

Plzeňská

Kartouzská

Štefánikova

Plzeňská

Duškova

Mozartova

Radlická

Stroupežnické

Vrchlického

Na Zatlance

Kováků

Villa Bertramka (Mozart Museum) ▶ ▶

Erbenova

*Façade of the Church
of Our Lady Victorious.*

Church of Our Lady Victorious (*Kostel Panny Marie Vitězné*) - The name of the church recalls the victorious Battle of the White Mountain when the Catholic League triumphed over Protestant troops on 8th November 1620. The church, which was completed by the Italian architect G.M. Filippi in the first half of the 17th century, is considered to be the first Baroque church in Prague. It stands in *Karmelitská* street and its **interior**, modelled on the Gesù Church in Rome, is famous for the much revered *Statue of the Holy Infant of Prague* ("Jezulátko"). This small wax figure (50 cm), situated on the right-hand wall of the church, was brought from Spain as a gift from Princess Polyxena of Lobkowitz in 1628. The 18th century altar bears statues by P. Prachner, and a silver casket of the

Church of Our Lady Victorious, Statue of the Holy Infant of Prague.

View of the Petřín Observation Tower.

Holy Infant of the same era. The 18th century high altar is the work of followers of J.F. Schor. Underneath the church lie the **Catacombs** (closed to the public), with mummified remains of Carmelite friars and their benefactors.

Italian Hospital (*Nemocnice Pod Petřínem*) - Located in the upper part of the wooded Petřín hill, this building is now an integral part of the Italian Embassy in Prague. It houses the Cultural Institute, where courses in Italian are organised. This spot used to be the site of a hospital serving the substantial Italian community which had settled in the city in the 16th century and which included architects, artists, merchants and ordinary workers, attracted by the period of development under way in Prague in the Baroque era.

Petřín Observation Tower (*Petřínská rozhledna*) - The fact that Prague is often defined as the "Paris of the East" by travel publications is only partly due to the pleasant nature of its monuments and localities; the term also derives from this iron tower which was built for the Prague Industrial Exhibition in 1891 as an imitation of the Parisian Eiffel Tower. It is 60m tall and now used as a television tower. Unlike its French counterpart, the climb to the top has to be made on foot (299 steps), but the view is well worth the effort: on a clear day the "Golden City", its hills and the surrounding areas are all visible.

The Mirror Maze viewed from the Petřín Observation Tower.

Mirror Maze (*Bludiště*) - The maze is housed in an attractive pavilion which also contains a wooden model of the Charles Gate, and a diorama of *The Defence of Prague against the Swedes in 1648*. The painting is by A. Liebscher and V. Bartoněk (end of 19th century). The Mirror Maze was built at the same time as the Observation Tower and is one of Petřín hill's attractions.

Church of St Lawrence (*Kostel svatého Vavřince*) - The present Baroque appearance of this place of worship dates back to the 18th century when an earlier Romanesque building, first recorded in the mid-12th century, was reconstructed by I. Palliardi. The **façade** is enriched with a 19th century *Statue of St Adalbert*, the work of F. Dvořáček. Inside the church note the late 17th century painting above the high altar showing *The Torment of St Adalbert*, by J.C. Monnos. The Sacristy ceiling is decorated with an 18th century fresco illustrating *The Legend of the Foundation of the Church of St Adalbert*.

Observatory (*Hvězdárna*) - The observatory houses the Czech Academy of Science's Astronomical Institute. Part of the building was opened to the public for the first time in 1928. Guided tours and astronomical events are organised for those interested in this subject. The collection of telescopes used for observations ranges from the modern instrument to models now obsolete.

Villa Bertramka, home to the Mozart Museum.

Villa Bertramka (***Bertramka***) - The villa dates from the 17th century and has had various owners. In the second half of the 18th century it belonged to the Dušeks, with whom W.A. Mozart often stayed, composing and attending some of the debut performances of his works. This Prague residence of Mozart's is situated at the foot of a wooded hill with a magnificent park behind it.

Mozart Museum - Named after the great Salzburg composer, the museum was founded around the middle of the 19th century by the Popelkas, father and son. It is arranged on the first floor of the Villa Bertramka and was opened in 1956. Along with the Smetana and Dvořák museums, it forms the *National Museum's Independent Section of Musicology*. Note the *Bust of Mozart* by T. Seidan set in the villa's gardens. Of particular interest, besides the composer's study and bedroom, are some of the music scores, letters and historic concert posters. Concerts are held in the villa.

THE LORETO AREA

LORETO - CAPUCHIN MONASTERY - NEW WORLD - CHURCH OF ST JOHN NEPOMUK - CZERNIN PALACE - **STRAHOV MONASTERY**

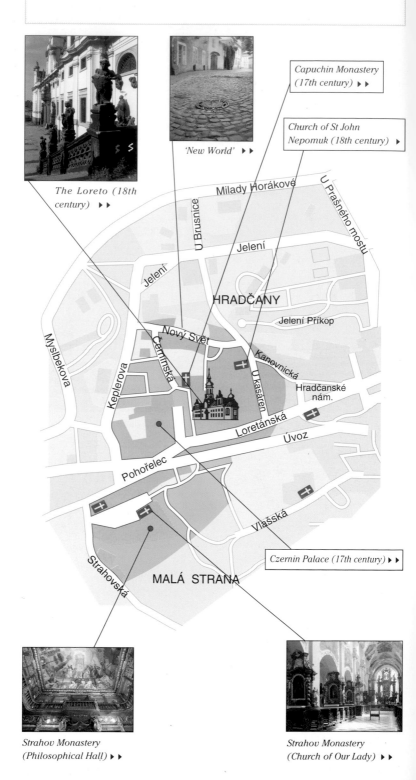

The Loreto (18th century) ▶ ▶

'New World' ▶ ▶

Capuchin Monastery (17th century) ▶ ▶

Church of St John Nepomuk (18th century) ▶

Czernin Palace (17th century) ▶ ▶

Strahov Monastery (Philosophical Hall) ▶ ▶

Strahov Monastery (Church of Our Lady) ▶ ▶

The Loreto (*Loreta*) - The origins of this sanctuary, which ranks as one of the most visited religious destinations and places of pilgrimage in the whole of Bohemia, date back to the 18th century, although the legend which tells of the transportation of the Santa Casa from Nazareth to Loreto is much older (13th century). Following the Counter-Reformation, a great number of sanctuaries modelled on the one in Loreto were built, in order to promote Catholicism in the previously Protestant areas. The **façade** of the sanctuary was begun after 1721 by the Dientzenhofers, who had been commissioned by the Prince of Lobkowitz and his wife Eleanor Caroline. The main entrance is distinguished by the statues of *Saints* and the marble coats of arms which stand above it, all by F. Kohl. The Baroque bell tower houses a set of 27 bells (1694) which ring out in honour of the Virgin every hour in summer. The **Santa Casa Chapel** was completed in the first half of the 17th century by G.B. Orsi from Como. It is found in the Cloisters, surrounded by porticoes and decorated with two fountains. The external decorations are either inspired by *Episodes from the Life of the Virgin Mary,* the *Legend of the Santa Casa,* or represent *Prophets from the Old Testament* and *Pagan Sibyls.* The **interior** of the chapel, which is beautifully painted by the 17th century Malá Strana artist, F. Kunz, contains an ornate silver altar, a wooden *Madonna,* and various silver decorations weighing a total of over 50kg. The atmosphere inside is tranquil and enchanting; a splendid iconostasis stands before the image of the Virgin Mary. On either side of the Santa Casa are two 18th century fountains representing the *Assumption* and the *Resurrection.* The **Cloister** dates from the first half of the 17th century and is adorned with 18th century frescoes by

View of the Loreto.

Detail of the elaborate façade of the Loreto.

F.A. Scheffler. The chapels which surround the cloister are rich with frescoes, paintings and sculptures, and they are distinguished by wooden confessionals and altar frontals of excellent craftsmanship. The construction of the **Church of the Nativity**, situated on the eastern side of the Loreto, halfway along the cloister, was begun by the Dientzenhofer father and son team in 1717, and completed by G. Aichbauer in 1735. The **interior** is a genuine triumph of Baroque, with its incredible wealth of decorations including sculptures, wooden inlay work, gold-leafed stuccowork, painted vaulting, angels and *putti*, and multi-coloured marble. The high altar is adorned with an altar-piece by J.G. Heintsch (*Nativity),* and there are numerous frescoes including *Christ in the Temple,* on the ceiling, (V.V. Reiner, 18th century) and *Adoration of the Shepherds, Adoration of the Magi* (J.A. Schöpf, 18th century). It is also worth visiting the interesting **Treasury**, situated in the upper passage of the cloister. It contains liturgical items, chasubles and some valuable 16th-18th century monstrances, including several exquisite examples, decorated with pearls, diamonds and other precious stones. Some of these priceless jewels were made in Vienna by J. Künischbauer and M. Stegner, jewellers to the Habsburg Court.

Capuchin Monastery (*Kapucínský klášter*) - This building with its plain features extends along the northern side of the *Loretánské námestí.* It was built at the beginning of the 17th century and was the first Capuchin monastery in Bohemia. An overhead covered passage connects it to the Loreto Sanctuary. Nearby is the simple **Church of the Madonna** which contains a cycle of Gothic panel-paintings.

New World (*Nový Svět*) - Not far from the Loreto complex is the "New World", which is in fact a quarter within a quarter, and certainly one of the most fascinating areas of Hradčany. It is the students' and artists' quarter, a kind of "Latin Quarter" on the banks of the Vtlava, in keeping with the stereotype of the "Paris of the East". The former home of the astronomer Kepler ("The House at the Golden Griffin") can be seen here, as well as an attractive Baroque *vinárna* ("At the Golden Pear").

Church of St John Nepomuk (*Kostel svatého Jana Nepomuckého*) - This church was built in the first half of the 18th century to support the nearby Ursuline Convent. The plans were drawn up by K.I. Dientzenhofer who, with this building, made his architectural debut in the capital. In the first half of the 19th century the tower was restructured. The **interior** contains some particularly interesting paintings which celebrate the saint. The ceiling paintings by V.V. Reiner represent the *Glorification of Life* and the *Miracle of St John Nepomuk.* Some 18th century altar-pieces by J.K. Liškas and M. Willmann, show *The Capture of the Saint.*

Czernin Palace (*Černínský palác*) - Now the seat of the Ministry of Foreign Affairs, the distinguishing marks of this majestic building are its imposing size and the massive colonnade which runs the length of the façade. The whole length of the ground floor level is constructed with massive diamond-pointed rustication. Work was begun on the palace in the second half of the 17th century by order of the Ambassador to Vienna, Count Czernin of Chudenice. It was completed towards the end of the century under the supervision of the diplomat's son, Hermann Czernin. The many eminent Italian artists who took part in the construction of the palace made some outstanding contributions, among whom was F. Caratti. In the first half of the 18th century the adjoining garden was added, as was the magnificent stairway with its ceiling fresco by V.V. Reiner (*Fall of the Titans*). During the same period, F.M. Kaňka made some adjustments to the building. Towards the middle of the 18th century renovation work was needed, following the French occupation, and this was carried out by A. Lurago who added three doorways and rebuilt the garden *Orangery* in Rococo style. Around this time I.F. Platzer produced several sculptures which now decorate the palace halls.

The imposing façade of Czernin Palace.

Strahov Monastery (*Strahovský klášter*) - This building, founded by the Premonstratensians, dates from the 12th century when it was built under the patronage of Duke Vladislav II and the Bishop of Olomouc. In 1258 it was destroyed by fire and rebuilt in Gothic style. In the second half of the 14th century, Charles IV had the building included within the walls of Prague. It was considerably extended and embellished during the Renaissance period, but destroyed by the Swedes at the end of the Thirty Years' War. The architect J.B. Mathey remodelled the monastery complex in Baroque style in the second half of the 17th century. Damaged once again by the events of war (1741), it rose to its former splendour in the neo-classical period. In the early 1950s restoration work brought to light the remains of the Romanesque foundations. In the courtyard there is a Baroque gateway, above which stands the *Statue of St Norbert,* the founder of the Premonstratensians. Rudolph II had the former Chapel of St Roch built in the first half of the 17th century; today it is used for exhibitions. Behind the 17th century *Column of St Norbert* lies the **Church of Our Lady**, also dating from the 17th century. Above the harmonious Baroque **façade** stands a *Lamb*, surrounded by the golden epigraph *Vidi supra Montem Sion Agnum.* The **interior** is divided into three naves and is richly decorated in Baroque style; it contains some fine furnishings (scrolls in stuccowork with images of the Virgin Mary). Next to the church is the part of the monastery which houses the **Museum of National Literature (*Památník národního písemnictví*).** The monastery's Historical Library, now once again in the possession of the monks (1992), contains 130,000 volumes, 5000 manuscripts, 2500 incunabula and a large quantity of old maps. It also houses examples of Czech literature from the 9th to the 18th centuries. The Library's *Theological Hall* is of particular interest for its fine stuccowork and its 18th century paintings. The barrel vaulting, clearly Baroque in style, is the work of G.D. Orsi of Orsini. The cycle of 25 frescoes by S. Nosecký, the Strahov monk, is a masterpiece in itself. The *Philosophical Hall* is of remarkable dimensions, corresponding to the size of the bookcases which it holds. The large ceiling fresco was painted in the 18th century by F.A. Maulpertsch. Also on display in the hall is a *Bust*

Strahov Monastery from Petřín Observation Tower.

Strahov Monastery, façade of the Church of Our Lady.

of Francis I, made in marble by F.X. Lederer in the 19th century. The most notable items in the library, those which constitute its wealth, are the valuable *Strahov Gospel Book* (9th-10th century), the *Historia Anglorum,* the *Schelmenberg Bible,* and the *Strahov Herbarium.*

Strahov Monastery, Theological Hall.

On the next page:
Strahov Monastery, Philosophical Hall.

THE ŽIŽKOV AND TROJA AREAS

Prague Museum - National Monument of Žižkov - Television Tower - Troja Palace

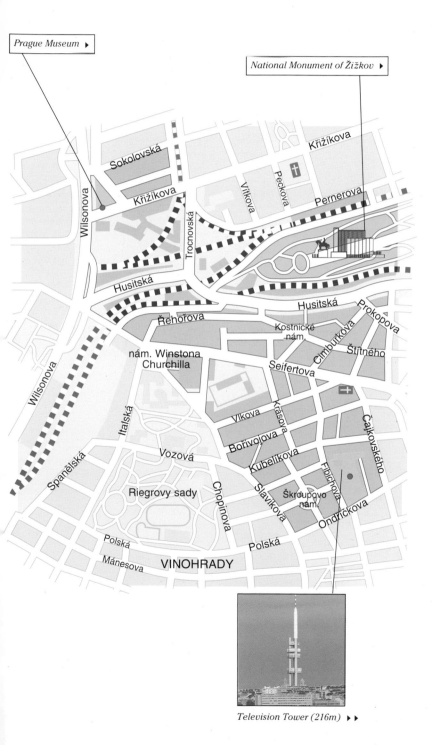

Prague Museum ▸

National Monument of Žižkov ▸

Sokolovská
Křižíkova
Wilsonova
Vítkova
Peckova
Křižíkova
Pernerova
Trocnovská
Husitská
Husitská
Prokopova
Řehořova
Kostnické nám.
Cimburkova
Štítného
nám. Winstona Churchilla
Seifertova
Wilsonova
Italská
Vlkova
Krásova
Čajkovského
Španělská
Bořivojova
Vozová
Kubelíkova
Fibichova
Riegrovy sady
Chopinova
Slavíkova
Škroupovo nám.
Ondříčkova
Polská
Polská
Mánesova
VINOHRADY

Television Tower (216m) ▸▸

Prague Museum (*Muzeum hlavního města Prahy*) - The neo-Renaissance building which houses the museum was erected towards the end of the 19th century to a design by A. Balšánek and A. Wiehl. The **façade** is decorated with sculptures by various artists, and above the staircase hangs the face from the Old Town Hall Astronomical Clock showing the months of the year by J. Mánes, who also painted the *Signs of the Zodiac*. The *tondi* in the outer ring are inspired by *The Annual Cycle*. The Museum's collections offer an interesting view of the city's urban, architectural, cultural and economic history. The model of the city as it was in the early 19th century deserves special attention. It gives a reliable indication of the urban reorganisation work carried out in the historical centre and the Jewish quarter, and the size of the model (20m²) and the great care given to the detail of buildings and architectural features is extraordinary. It was made in 1830 by the lithographer A. Langweil. Other exhibits worthy of note in the museum's collection include historic costumes, jewellery, sculptures, china and furnishings, as well as a substantial collection of attractive house signs.

National Monument of Žižkov (*Národní památník na Žižkové*) - This imposing monument is situated in the quarter of the same name, to the east of the city centre. It was built between the end of the 1920s and the beginning of the 1930s, while the interior was completed after 1948. At the top of the panoramic terrace stands the *Equestrian Statue of Jan Žižka,* the Hussite general, erected in 1950 by B. Kafka. Behind this stands the Monument, a grey, cold reminder of the past, built in reinforced concrete; it contains the bodies of important leaders of the old regime. Worthy of note is the *Memorial to the Victims of World War I,* and the *Tomb of the Unknown Soldier* from World War II. At the beginning of the road which

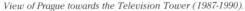

View of Prague towards the Television Tower (1987-1990).

leads from the *Husitská* to the Monument is the **Museum of Military History** containing documentation on World War II, and collections of weapons and uniforms.

Television Tower (*Televizní vysílac*) - The new television tower stands out clearly against the capital's urban landscape. The shape of the tower is rather unusual, and it stands 216m high with a panoramic restaurant at the top. The viewing platform can be reached by lift between 10am and 6pm daily.

Troja Palace ▶ ▶

Troja Palace (*Trojský zámek*) - This splendid Baroque palace ranks among the most beautiful summer residences in the capital. It is situated in the quarter of Troja, which lies to the north of the Vtlava, in the northern suburbs of Prague. The architect G.B. Mathey was commissioned to build the palace by Count Sternberg, one of the most well-known members of the city's aristocracy. Mathey completed the building between 1679 and 1685, modelling the exterior on the style of the Classical Italian villa. The magnificent staircase which leads down to the garden was added between 1685 and 1703. It has a double flight of steps and is decorated with mythological statues by Johann Georg, Paul Hermann, and the Brokoff brothers (*Sons of Mother Earth, Struggle between the Olympian Gods and the Titans*). Inside the building note the great *Imperial Hall,* decorated with beautiful frescoes by A. Godin showing the *Glory of the Habsburgs.* This Dutch artist, who worked on the hall's decoration, also painted the noteworthy *Personification of Justice.* The so-called *Chinese Rooms* contain a collection of ceramics

The lovely Troja Palace, the miniature Bohemian 'Versailles'.

and are decorated with 19th century wall paintings of Chinese scenes. The palace, which because of its imposing nature is also known as *Troja Castle,* is complemented by the beautiful and enchanting **Troja Gardens** *(Letohrádek Troja)*. These were designed by the architect Mathey, who in fact planned the entire complex; he made the gardens in a distinctly early-French Baroque style. From the *Orangerie*s at the bottom of the gardens, not far from the Vltava, there is a charming view of the whole of this miniature Bohemian "Versailles". Careful restoration work has restored The Troja palace and gardens to their former splendour. The palace contains a 19th century art collection.

Troja Palace, detail of the entrance staircase.

THE VYŠEHRAD AREA

Vyšehrad - Church of St Peter and St Paul - Cemetery - St Martin's Rotunda - Tabor Gate and Leopold Gate

Vyšehrad (view from the Vltava) ▶ ▶

St Martin's Rotunda
(11th-19th centuries) ▶ ▶

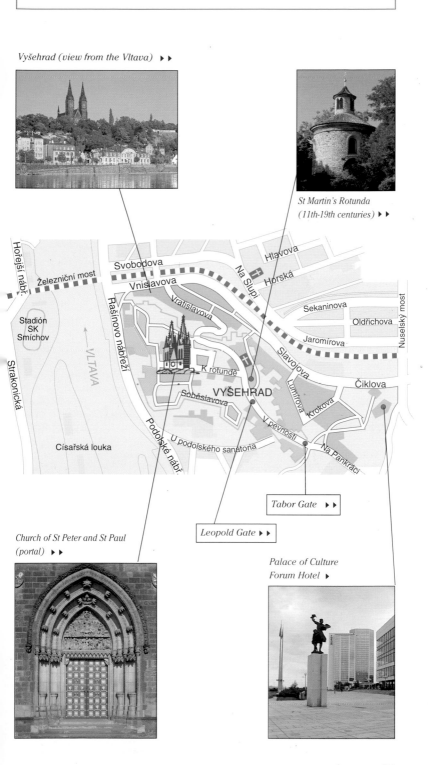

Tabor Gate ▶ ▶

Leopold Gate ▶ ▶

Church of St Peter and St Paul
(portal) ▶ ▶

Palace of Culture
Forum Hotel ▶

River view of Vyšehrad.

Vyšehrad - The meaning of Vyšehrad is "castle on the heights", and the hill where it is situated is said to have been the seat of the first Přemyslid princes. It was almost certainly founded in the 10th century as a rival to Hradčany Castle. From the 11th century onwards it became more and more important as sovereigns established themselves here, and the building was expanded. It went into a period of decline around the mid-12th century, and was fortified two centuries later. The settlement suffered greatly during The Hussite Wars (15th century). By the beginning of the 17th century the area had taken on the appearance of a Baroque fortress. After its destruction in 1911, Vyšehrad is today undergoing careful restoration work.

Church of St Peter and St Paul *(Kostel svatého Petra a Pavla)* - This church, situated on the heights of Vyšehrad, is a striking feature on Prague's skyline. Its twin spires dominate the houses which overlook the right bank of the Vtlava, making it one of the symbols of this quarter of the capital. The first place of worship on this site was built in the latter half of the 11th century. During the reign of Charles IV the church was rebuilt to become a three-naved basilica in distinctly Gothic style. It was subsequently remodelled in Renaissance style in the 16th century, and again in Baroque style in the 18th century. However, the church today offers the neo-Gothic appearance it assumed in the latter half of the 19th century. Further restoration work was carried out between 1981 and 1987, at the same time as some archaeological excavations. The **façade** of the church

Tabor Gate forms the entrance to the old quarter of Vyšehrad.

Church of St Peter and St Paul, detail of the portal doors.

is wedged between two soaring spires, erected in the early 20th century and jointly designed by J. Mocker and F. Mikš. The neo-Gothic appearance of the façade is reinforced by its triangular tympanum decorated with sculptures. The lunettes of the magnificent, deeply splayed portals are decorated with mosaics (side portals), and with high relief work (central portal). Note the doors themselves enriched with coats of arms and precious gold-leaf work. The **interior** contains some notable frescoes with stylised motives, dating from the early 1900s. The church's charm is enhanced by the beauty of the decorations and paintings which completely cover the naves and the ceiling (which is formed of ribbed cross-vaulting). Pillars supporting ogival arches separate the three naves. Above the side altars, themselves enriched with various works in wood (altar frontals, sculptures, triptychs), there are some finely illustrated windows. The high altar, by J. Mocker, is decorated with four statues by F. Hrubes (late 19th century); these represent *St Peter and St Paul, St Cyril and St Methodius.* Note also, in the first chapel on the right, the *Tomb of St Longinus,* an 11th century Romanesque stone sarcophagus, and in the third chapel on the right the 14th century panel painting of *Our Lady of the Rains.* Observe the fine wooden pulpit and the beautiful choir made of the same material.

Vyšehrad, view of the Cemetery.

Cemetery (*Vyšehradský hřbitov*) - Originally a medieval cemetery adjoining the Church of St Peter and St Paul, it was transformed into a memorial of Czech art and culture in the latter half of the 19th century. The famous figures buried here include the painter M. Aleš, the writers K. Čapek, B. Němcová and J. Neruda, and the composers A. Dvořák and B. Smetana. The *Slavín Chapel* contains the sculptors B. Kafka, J.V. Myslbek and L. Šaloun.

A feature of the fine St Martin's Rotunda.

St Martin's Rotunda (*Rotunda svatého Martina*) - This pretty circular chapel with a small side apse is considered to be the oldest building in Prague. It was in fact built, in Romanesque style, in the 11th century, probably on the site of a building from the previous century. It was lucky enough to be spared the devastation caused by the Hussite wars, and was later used as a powder magazine. The chapel was rebuilt in the latter half of the 19th century.

Tabor Gate / Leopold Gate (*Táborská Brána / Leopoldova Brána*) - These gates are situated in the perimeter wall of the old fortress from where there are some lovely views. Leopold Gate, which is very close to the Romanesque Rotunda, gives onto the *V. pevnosti,* and at the end of this stands the Baroque Tabor Gate, forming an impressive bastion of the fortified complex. Not far from here, near the Vyšehrad underground station, rises the futuristic complex of the **Palace of Culture** (also used for conferences) and the **Forum Hotel.** These two 20th century constructions, built in the 1980s, are valid examples of contemporary Czech architecture.

View of Leopold Gate.

ENTERTAINMENT

Frequent boat trips are available for those wishing to admire the city from the river. These depart from the *Rašinovo nábřeží* quay. Short river cruises are also possible, complete with live folk music and the chance to sample specialities of Bohemian confectionery, served with coffee or excellent local beer. Excursions by boat are also available to the most popular tourist destinations of the surrounding area.

A tourist boat on the Vltava.

An evening can be spent in one of the typical *vinárny,* where you can try out Bohemian cooking and enjoy folk music and dancing.

During the tourist season concerts of classical music are held in many of the city's churches and palaces. Pamphlets giving details of each evening's programme are handed out in the streets.

One of the most interesting forms of theatre on offer is the "Black Theatre", a performance of mime through music, lights and dance:

Laterna Magica, *Národní 4*
Theatre Image, *Pařížská 4*

There is a good choice of theatre entertainment offering both opera and plays:

Národní divadlo, *Národní 2*
Stavovské divadlo, *Ovocný thr 1*
Státní opera Praha, *Wilsonova třída 4*

For lovers of night life Prague has a wealth of nightclubs, discotheques, and casinos. The following are only a selection of those on offer:

Cold Fingers + Alhambra, *Václavské náměstí 5*
Esplanade - Est Bar, *Washingtonova 19*
Diplomat - Skyline, *Evropská 15*
U Fleků, *Křemencová 9*
International - Račia, *Koulova 15*
Panorama, *Milevská 7*
Radost Fx, *Bělehradská 120*
Music Park, *Francouzská 4*
Variete Praga, *Vodičkova 30*
Casino Club 21, *Štefánikova 7*
Casino Palais Savarin, *Na příkopě 10*
Casino Admiral Praha, *5 května 65*

SHOPPING

Alongside the sightseeing, you will find shopping in Prague an enjoyable pastime. Favourable exchange rates encourage spending, and the goods on offer are extremely tempting. Be careful not to exceed in your purchases, or you may have trouble with customs when leaving the country. Bohemian crystal obviously accounts for the largest part of local products, although traditional crafts also include the noteworthy hand-painted wooden eggs decorated with religious designs and available in various sizes and at various prices. Also on offer are some lovely, carefully hand-painted wooden caskets. Alongside the crystal (especially lead crystal), the beautiful and excellently crafted Bohemian china also deserves a special mention. One of the most unusual items are the houses of Prague made of china. Wooden puppets, dolls in Bohemian folk costumes, delicately hand-painted Russian Dolls in various sizes, fabrics, shirts, and the inevitable T-shirts printed with symbols and images of Prague and Bohemia all make for a difficult choice. Apart from the usual range of "Kitsch" objects, we should also mention, for the sake of curiosity, the memorabilia from the old regime, including badges, insignia, military berets and uniforms.

Artists on Charles Bridge.

The shopping area is concentrated along *Karlova*, in the streets leading off *Staroměstské náměstí*, and in the "Golden Cross" (*Na příkopě, Ul. 28 října, Na můstku, Václavské náměstí*). A well-stocked souvenir and arts and crafts market is held in *Havelská* and the adjacent streets. In the Malá Strana quarter the *Nerudova* is good for shopping, as is the famous "Golden Lane" at the Castle.

The city's department stores include the following:

Bílá Labuť, *Na Poříčí 23; Václavské náměstí 59*
K Mart, *Národní 26*
Kotva, *Náměstí Republiky 8*

WHAT TO EAT AND DRINK, LOCAL DISHES, RESTAURANTS

B ohemian cuisine is very tasty, partly because of the liberal use made of sauces, herbs and spices. Its most popular dishes are very similar to those eaten in German-speaking countries and in Central Europe in general. The main dish, usually plentiful and well-garnished, is rather rich, not only because of the choice of dressings (olive oil is not very common here), but also the ingredients themselves. In fact, Czech cooking's speciality is pork, served in a whole range of ways. It is often accompanied by dumplings made with flour or potatoes, or with plain rice and plenty of gravy. On the subject of dumplings: do not expect the traditional Italian "*gnocchi*"; Czech dumplings are more like the "*canederli*" in Trentino cooking or Knödel from the South Tyrol region and in German cooking. They are a Bohemian speciality and are served cut into slices. I would recommend the dumplings with bacon (known as *Speckknödel* in German. It is always a good idea to ask for a menu written in German or English, unless of course you can understand Czech). Beef is usually stewed, and other common dishes are loin of pork, various kinds of sausages (würstel), chicken and game. Duck and goose are reserved for special occasions, while fish dishes, though much more difficult to find, usually consist of salmon, trout and the traditional Christmas carp. Do not expect vegetables or salads, but make do with rice or the above-mentioned dumplings. The latter also play an important part in the desserts department: they are made with plums, apricots, cranberries, apples and cherries. The *palačinky* deserve a special mention: a mouth-watering Bohemian version of the French *crêpe,* they are filled with peaches, cheese or jam and covered in melted chocolate.

As for what to drink, Prague claims to be the world beer capital, and rightly so. There is an enormous range of both light and dark beers available, of varying alcoholic content, fermentation process and method of production. Both local and Moravian and Slovakian wines are the most commonly served drinks in the *Vinárny,* but international wines and spirits (vodka, slivovice - plum brandy -, and various kinds of aqua vitae) are also served. Soft drinks (mineral water, orange, apple and grapefruit juice, and "Coca Cola") are available on request. The traditional Italian "espresso" coffee is widely available on request, as is normal, German-type coffee.

A Selection of Restaurants
U Bílého Koníka, *Karlova 7*
U Laury, *Nerudova 10*
Bohemia, *Václavské náměstí 21*
Hanavský Pavilon, *Letenské sady 173*
Pelikán, *Na příkopě 7*
Nebozízek, *Petrínské sady 411*
Parnas, *Smetanovo nábřeží 2*
U Lorety, *Loretánské náměstí 8*
U Tří Pštrosu, *Dražichého náměstí 6*
U Červeného Lva, *Nerudova 41*

A Selection of Vinárny
U Pavouka, *Celetná 17*
U Mecenáše, *Malostranské náměstí 10*
U Zelené Záby, *U radnice 8*
U Labutí, *Hradcanské námestí 11*
Sidi, *Na Kampe 10*
U Císarů, *Loretánská 175/5*
U Vladare, *Maltézské náměstí 10*
Blatnice, *Michalská 6-8*
U Zlaté Studně, *Karlova 3*
Velehradská Vinárna, *Velehradská 18*

WHERE TO STAY

I t is always advisable to book in advance. Prague's hotels are divided into five categories, from one star * to five stars *****. Leaving aside the "deluxe" and first class hotels, the standard of accommodation is usually good.

A Selection of Hotels
Esplanade *****, *Washingtonova 19*
Intercontinental *****, *Náměstí Curieových*
Jalta *****, *Václavské náměstí 45*
Savoy *****, *Keplerova 6*
Parkhotel ****, *Veletržní 20*
Forum ****, *Kongresová 1*
Evropa ****, *Václavské náměstí 25*
Diplomat ****, *Evropská 15*
Alta Praha ***, *Ortenovo náměstí 22*
Atlantic ***, *Na Poříčí*
Aron ***, *Žerotínova 1147/39*
Meteor **, *Hybernská 6*
Vítkov **, *Konenova 114*
Sporthotel Oaza **, *Jeremenkova 106*
Opera **, *Těšnov 13*

Magnificent view over Prague and her bridges.

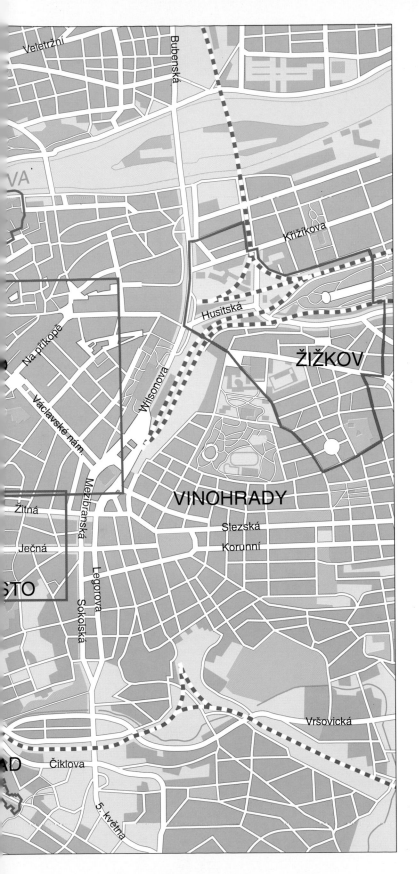

Veletržní
Bubenská
VA
Křižíkova
Na příkopě
Husitská
Wilsonova
ŽIŽKOV
Václavské nám.
Mezibranská
VINOHRADY
Žitná
Slezská
Ječná
Korunní
ŠTO
Legerova
Sokolská
Vršovická
AD
Čiklova
5. května

INDEX